D1567834

Civil War Cookin', Stories, 'n Such

by Darlene Funkhouser

Reprinted in 2001, 2002, 2003, 2004, 2005, 2007, 2010, 2013, 2014, 2015 and 2017

DEDICATION

This book is dedicated to the memory of my father, Austin Frederick Funkhouser (Cpl, U.S. Army Air Corps-WWII). He was a true Virginia gentleman and an avid student of The War Between the States.
This one's for you, Daddy!

ACKNOWLEDGMENTS

To Reverand Harold Burnette of St. Paul's Lutheran Church, Edinburg, VA, for potential leads;

To my editor, Bruce Carlson, for expert guidance and his wonderful sense of humor;

To my Uncle Danny (First Class Petty Officer James Daniel Carter, USN, Ret) for his knowledge of Naval warfare;

To Cedar Creek's Ninth Annual Reenactment in October, 1998;

To Lt. Commander Jeffrey Friar, USN for his input;

To Clita Graham, who tells some of
the best stories I've ever heard;

To my buddy, Joseph Shadrick (thanks
for the history book, Joe!),

To Tim Williams at Gatorland in
Orlando, Florida, ("The Alligator Capital
of the World") for his amazing knowledge
of gators;

To folks at New Market Battlefield
Museum, The Baltimore Civil War Museum,
Baltimore's Hampton Mansion, and The
Stonewall Jackson Museum (Strasburg, VA);

To Riviera Beach, Maryland librarians
Tim Burall, Peter England, Jill Hagen and
Janet Kreps for splendid research help
and their unfailing good nature;

To my good and patient friend,
Dr. David Bonnett who joined me on many
trips to uncover facts about the Civil
War. About half the photographs in this
book were taken by Dave;

And last but not least, sincere
thanks, gratitude and love go to my
mother, Millie Catherine Funkhouser.
She was the best mother a writer could
have.

Soups & Stews

Breads

Meat, Poultry & Seafood

Side Dishes

Desserts

The photographs in this book are all modern from the author's private collection. They were taken at various battlefields, re-enactments and other historical sites.

BROTHER AGAINST BROTHER

The Civil War, or the War Between the States as the C.S.A. knew it, cost the lives of more men than any other war in America's history. 620,000 men died. Not all were killed in battle; diseases -- measles, pneumonia, bronchitis, dysentery -- killed twice as many solidiers as battle. Gangrene was rampant, and 50,000 men returned home with amputations.

In border states Delaware, Maryland, Kentucky, Missouri and West Virginia, loyalties were heatedly divided. Maryland was forced to stay in the Union -- Lincoln could not afford to have the U.S. capital in the midst of the Confederacy. West Virginia

C.S.A. Surgeon
Cedar Creek, 1998

became a border state halfway through the war when western counties of Virginia sympathized with the Union and broke away. Virginia was the site of the most Civil War battles, and also held the most slaves.

Border states had soldiers who fought for either side, often pitting brother against brother. Border states did not produce the only divided loyalties -- 100,000 Southerners fought for the Union cause, and Northerners sometimes fought for the Confederacy.

MORE DISAGREEMENTS --

The two sides sometimes could not agree on what to call battles. The Battles of Bull Run were unknown to the C.S.A., which knew these fights to protect their capital city of Richmond as First and Second Manassas.

The Union was positive the war would be over quickly and the Confederates would scamper back home. The First Battle of Manassas brought out droves of Washingtonians on a hot summer Sunday. Merry folks

came to witness rebel defeat, spreading picnics on a
grassy knoll overlooking the battlefield.

BULL RUN BATTLEFIELD

Spectators scattered like dry leaves in a brisk wind
as the battle heated up and fiery rebels claimed
victory.
      Another battle was called Antietam in the
North, but the South called it Sharpsburg. Name
differences in battles came about because the North
often named battles after a creek or river near
battle sites; the South named the same battles after
the nearest town.
      At Antietam, Lee's hopes of gaining a
stronghold in the North (with the ultimate plan of
invading Washington, D.C.) were dashed by a lucky
Union break. A Union soldier came across a bundle of
cigars on the ground. Delighted by his find, he
eagerly tore the wrapping off the cigars. Lee's
secret order for gaining a Northern foothold
fluttered to the ground. Following this awesome
discovery, the hellish Battle of Antietam roared to
life hours later.
      The fighting around Antietam yielded strange
occurences. In Maryland days before Antietam, the
Battle of South Mountain was fought. People say that

on a hill nearby, Confederate ghosts lurk. If powder
is sprinkled on a car trunk and the car is put into
neutral, the fallen soldiers will push the car up the
hill. Handprints can be seen in the powder afterward.

At Antietam at twilight, folks say that
ghostly campfires can be seen on the forlorn killing
fields. Others tell eerie tales about resolute
soldiers marching along the creek bed.

Other people tell a
chilling account of a
bearded Confederate
officer astride a fine
horse one night. The horse
reared when it saw the
the people. The handsome
officer beckoned the
people with his eyes as he
rode into a barn. The people ran after horse and
rider, but the barn was empty... or **was** it?

SOUPS AND STEWS

Soups and stews were a perfect way for cooks to stretch meager food. Soups were often an entire meal. A clever cook could feed a whole camp on a few ingredients -- bellies might still rumble, but the edge was taken off.

ALLIGATOR STEW

Southern boys ate **anything** that walked, crawled, swam or flew, and gators were no exception. Gator killing was popular during the 1800's -- farmboys shot them from riverbanks, competing to see who could bag the largest gator. Gators range in size from ten to fourteen feet. Meat was taken from the tail,

Very young gators -- three and four feet long. Any gator less than six feet was not worth eating. Gatorland, Orlando

legs and sides. The only thing to remember was to be darned **sure** the gator was dead before fixing him for supper -- gators are a notoriously snappish lot when aggravated.

Recipe:
Meat from a gator's tail, legs and sides
Any vegetables you have on hand
Salt and pepper

Cut gator meat into bite-sized chunks. Cook in water 1-1¼ hours (until meat is tender). Add vegetables about 20 minutes before gator is done.

16

BEAN SOUP

1 lb navy or pinto beans (any beans will do)
onion, chopped
a couple of potatoes, peeled and diced
carrots, diced (if you have them)
4 or 5 tomatoes (if you have them)
ham (if available)
salt and pepper

Soak beans overnight, drain off soaking water, add
fresh water, cook until beans are soft, 1-1½ hours.
Cook ham with beans. Add vegetables 20 minutes
before the end of cooking.

BEEF STEW

beef - however much you can find
3 carrots, chopped
3 celery stalks, chopped (if available)
2 or 3 onions, chopped
5 or 6 potatoes, peeled and cut up
2 or 3 turnips or parsnips (if available),
    cut up
salt and pepper

Cube beef, put in a large pot. Add vegetables,
cover with water, simmer for about 1½ hours. Stir
from time to time, making sure there is enough
water.

BRUNSWICK STEW

1 squirrel, dressed and cut into pieces
1 chicken, dressed and cut into pieces
2 large onions, chopped
1 pound of potatoes, peeled and diced
4 or 5 tomatoes, chopped
salt and pepper
corn kernels from 5 or 6 ears of corn
3 or 4 carrots, diced (if available)

Cook the chicken and squirrel in a Dutch oven;
first, bring water to a boil, then reduce heat
and simmer chicken and squirrel 1½-2 hours
(until tender). When chicken and squirrel
have cooled, remove meat from the bones.

Return meat to pot; add vegetables (except
the corn) and simmer for ½ hour. During the
last ten minutes, add corn.

BURGOO

Burgoo (for which Kentucky claims credit) is a stewy mishmash of all meats on hand. <u>Any</u> old combination will do. Burgoo is a splendid way to get rid of leftover scraps before meat spoils.

Some folks claim that when being served a steaming bowl of burgoo, they see in the murky brown water an unsettling combination of feathers, fur, claws, eyes and fangs. At that point, eating the entire bowl of burgoo becomes more a proof of manhood than anything else.

Recipe:
Meat (you name it -- squirrel, possum, rabbit, beef, mutton, chicken, turkey, fish, ???)
2 large onions, chopped
4 large potatoes, peeled and in large chunks
3 or 4 tomatoes, peeled, chopped, with juice
ears of corn (however many you might have), cooked and kernels scraped from cob
Any other vegetables on hand (why not?)

If meats are not cooked, cook them by dredging in flour and browning them in a skillet with lard or bacon grease.

Transfer meats to a Dutch oven or a large pot, add boiling water. Add vegetables (except tomatoes and corn), cover the pot, reduce heat, and let the whole concoction simmer for $1\frac{1}{2}$ hours. Add the corn and tomatoes, cover and simmer another 45-60 minutes.

CABBAGE SOUP

4 tbs butter or lard
2 potatoes, peeled and
    diced
1 large onion, chopped
4½ C water
1 head of cabbage
salt and pepper

Cook potato and onion
in butter until
tender (10 minutes).
Peel outer leaves off
cabbage, cut out
thick stems. Peel
layers until the core
is reached; dispose of
core. Chop leaves
into 1½-2 inch
pieces. Add cabbage
to other items, cook
just until cabbage is
tender (no more than
10 minutes). Do not
overcook.

FISH SOUP

Bones from 4-5 fish - any kind of fish will do
4-5 fish, cleaned and cut up into chunks
8 C water
2 chopped onions
6-8 potatoes, peeled and diced
4 celery stalks, diced (if available)
3 tomatoes, chopped with liquid
salt and pepper

   In large pot, combine fish bones, water and
salt. Bring to boil, reduce heat, simmer 30 minutes.
Strain into a clean pot, throw bones away. Add
everything except fish, reduce heat, simmer 15
minutes. Add fish, cook 15 more minutes.

CHICKEN NOODLE SOUP

1 good-sized chicken
2 onions, diced
3 celery stalks, diced
3 carrots, sliced
4 quarts water
salt and pepper

Clean and cut chicken into bite-sized pieces.
Throw everything into a pot. Cook soup 2-2½ hours.
Add noodles, cook 15 minutes longer.

NOODLES:

2 eggs, beaten
1 C flour
½ tsp salt

   Add salt to eggs and flour. Roll or pat
very thin, let dry. Cut into thin strips. Cook 15
minutes in boiling chicken pot. If noodles will be
served alone, cook for 15 minutes in boiling water.

HAM AND COLLARDS SOUP

2 quarts water
ham pieces - as many as you
   have left over (or a
   healthy-sized fresh
   piece)
2 bunches of collard
   greens, stems removed
black-eyed peas or rice,
   cooked (if available)
salt and pepper

     Bring water to a boil.
If ham is not cooked, cook
in boiling water one hour.
Wash greens until sand is
gone. Add greens to ham,
cook for 30 minutes (don't
let water boil off). Add
peas or rice, heat to hot,
add salt and pepper.

NOTE: This soup is fine
without ham. Turnip
greens could take the
place of collards.

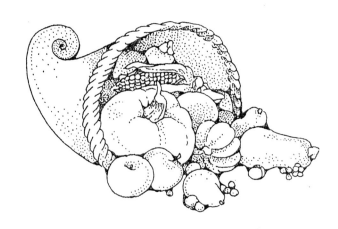

MUTTON STEW

Almost any available vegetables would do in this stew. Mutton smells pretty bad when it is being cooked, and the strong flavor is almost an acquired taste.

mutton - cut into 1½-inch cubes
flour
potatoes
carrots
turnips or parsnips
cabbage leaves, chopped coarsely
green beans
lard
water
salt and pepper

Dredge mutton cubes in flour and brown them in hot lard in a Dutch oven. Add water to cover meat with two to three inches over the top of the meat. Bring to a boil, cover, reduce heat and simmer for 1¼ hours. Add vegetables and simmer 40-45 minutes longer.

OKRA AND HAM GUMBO

Gumbos were cooked by Southern troops -- gumbos were easy to make, and could use ham, chicken, or oysters.

2 tbs bacon grease, lard or butter
ham (however much is on hand)
1 onion, chopped
2 or 3 tomatoes, chopped
2-3 C okra, sliced
2 or 3 potatoes, peeled and diced
celery, diced (if available)
2 or 3 ears of corn, scraped from cob (if
  available)
salt and pepper
water

Cook onion in grease in a pot for five minutes. Add everything else; boil for 2 or 3 minutes. Reduce to simmer, cover the pot and cook 30-40 minutes. Do not overcook.

OXTAIL SOUP

3 pounds oxtail, cut in 2 inch pieces
flour
2 tbs lard
10 C water
3 carrots, diced
3 stalks celery, diced (if available)
2 or 3 diced turnips or parsnips (if available)
salt and pepper

Dredge oxtails in flour, heat lard in a soup pot and brown oxtails. Remove oxtails, add water to pot and return meat to pot. Partially cover pot and simmer 2½ hours (until meat is tender), replacing any water that evaporates. Strain soup, remove meat from bones return meat to the soup. Add vegetables and simmer another 30 minutes.

OYSTER STEW

shucked oysters - as many as you have on hand,
    cut into bite-sized pieces
1 C onion, chopped
1 C celery, diced
5 or 6 potatoes, peeled and diced
6 C milk (or you can substitute ½ the milk with
    water, although all-milk is much better)
salt and pepper
butter or lard

Saute onion and celery in butter or lard until
tender (about five minutes). Add potatoes and
the other ingredients (except oysters). Bring
to a boil over a medium heat, then reduce heat
and cook for 20-25 minutes. Add oysters and cook
3-5 minutes.

PEANUT SOUP

    Peanuts (goobers) were common during the
War. They like hot weather, so the South was most
likely to make peanut soup.

1 C peanuts
1 small onion, chopped
1 tbs butter
3 C water
salt and pepper

Chop peanuts up pretty fine, set aside. In a pot,
cook the onion in butter for five minutes. Stir
peanuts into the butter, add everything else, bring
to a boil. Reduce heat and simmer over low heat
about half an hour.

POTATO SOUP

This is a "make-do" soup. If potatoes were the only vegetable available, the other vegetables would not be missed too much.

4 tbs butter
3 stalks celery, chopped
Potatoes, as many as
  needed, peeled and diced
5 or 6 C milk*

1 or 2 onions, chopped
2 or 3 C water
2 or 3 chopped carrots
salt and pepper

*If there is not enough milk, more water has to do.

Heat butter in a large pot and cook onions, carrots and celery about 15 minutes, stirring once in a while. Add potatoes, milk, water and seasonings, reduce heat and cook 20 minutes (until potatoes are tender). Thicken soup by mashing a few dices against the inside of the pot; stir mashed potatoes into soup.

SQUIRREL STEW

4 squirrels, cleaned
2 C flour
12 tbs lard
4 C water
2 or 3 potatoes, peeled and cut up
2 or 3 carrots (if available)
1 onion, chopped
salt and pepper

Cut squirrels into bite-sized pieces. Mix salt and pepper in flour, dredge squirrel pieces in flour. In a Dutch oven, fry pieces in lard until golden brown. Remove squirrel; pour off fat (except a few tablespoons). Add water to Dutch oven, bring to a boil. Return squirrel to oven, bring to boil, reduce heat. Simmer $1\frac{1}{4}$ hours, add vegetables, simmer 20-30 minutes.

TOMATO SOUP

12 C water
20-24 tomatoes,
skinned and chopped
4 small onions,
chopped
salt and pepper
1 bay leaf (if
available)

Put ingredients in
a large pot; simmer
1-1½ hours.

TURKEY SOUP

Meat from a good-sized turkey cut into bite-sized
pieces
2 onions, chopped
2 or 3 carrots, chopped
2 or 3 celery stalks, chopped (if available)
water

If turkey is not already cooked, cook it in water for
1-1½ hours. Add vegetables, cook an additional 15
minutes.

TURTLE SOUP

If you get hold of a snapping turtle, hold out a tree branch or a very thick stick and let him snap on to that -- he won't let go, and no humans should get bitten.

No one wants to end up like the small boy who found a snapping turtle and claimed it as a pet. His mother warned him to leave it alone. Soon she heard a scream, and she ran outside. The turtle had snapped on to his nose. The entire family's best efforts could not make the beast release his hold, so they all rushed to the emergency room (the second home of many boys).

There, doctors and nurses labored to release the turtle's maniacal hold (while no doubt trying to keep straight faces). The reptile's stubbornness did him in, because medics cut his head off to release the lad's nose. They **then** had to deal with a little boy who was upset that his new pet was so gruesomely slain.
Morale: Exercise extreme caution when dealing with turtles.

Recipe:
1 large turtle
2 tbs salt
pepper
2 tbs butter
1 C milk (if available)

Cut head off, remove the shell. Remove skin and innards. Cut meat into cubes and put in large pot. Add four quarts of water and bring to a boil. Reduce heat, and cook slowly for two hours. Just before serving, add salt, pepper, butter and milk.

VENISON STEW

6 pounds venison, cubed in 2" pieces
4 tbs butter
3 onions, sliced
2 or 3 carrots, sliced
4 or 5 potatoes, peeled and cut up
2 or 3 turnips or parsnips, cut up (if available)

      In a Dutch oven, brown venison well in butter; add onion, cook five minutes. Completely cover venison with water, cover and simmer slowly, about 2 hours. During the last 30 minutes, add the vegetables.

A WAR OF FIRSTS, WEAPONRY,
AND THE NAVY

The Civil War was, in many ways, a modern war. It was the first war to use trench warfare, allowing its fighters **some** small measure of protection. A veteran of a much later war, WWII, told that forty minutes he spent in a foxhole under enemy fire were the longest forty minutes of his life. Trenches could not keep Civil War soldiers from feeling fear, but soldiers at least now had a way to escape enemy fire and/or detection. They had a **chance** to stay alive or avoid serious injury.

The War brought the first "dogtags," made from handkerchiefs or pieces of paper. These "tags" showing a soldier's name and address were pinned to uniforms.

The Civil War first used the concept of "total warfare". The most complete use of total warfare was, of course, Sherman's March Through Georgia, which cost Georgia $100,000,000. Total warfare called for not merely destroying as many enemy soldiers and gaining as much territory as possible, it called for destroying everything of the enemy's: farms, plantations, livestock, towns, cities, families. Nothing would be left once enemy soldiers barreled through. The idea was to demoralize the opponent -- bring him to his knees. Total warfare was so complete that the C.S.A. had a problem at the end of the war -- rebels deserted to get home to try to save their families from absolute chaos and ruin.

This war also saw the use of hydrogen observation balloons. These balloons were attached

30

to long ropes staked to the ground. The balloons
created artificial hills or vantage points from which
battle strategies could be devised. Observers from
high above could spot troop movement, and artillery
fire was made more accurate.

WEAPONRY:

Another Civil War first was the use of
repeating arms which fired several rounds without
reloading; these weapons proved invaluable. The
Sharps Carbine was the first successful repeating
rifle in the first
modern war. At the
beginning of the war,
smoothbore muskets were
used. Rifle muskets were
quickly developed, with
U.S. Models 1842/55 being
favored. Springfield
developed their 1855/61
rifle muskets, which with
a range of 600 yards, were
the favorite of both
sides. English Enfield
rifles and rifle muskets
were also prized by both
sides. Unfortunately,
infantrymen were not
able to use many of the
fancy new weapons --
the calvary mostly
received these arms.

Many C.S.A. soldiers liked a good sawed-off
double-barreled shotgun, and musketoons appeared on
both sides of the fence. Sharpshooters on both
sides preferred the British Whitworth Rifle (1,500
yards) and the Leonard Target Rifle (1,000 yards).

Colt came in heavily with handguns: the
Colt .44-caliber Army revolver was the undisputed
favorite sidearm, and the Colt .36-caliber revolver
ran a close second. The LeMat 9-shot revolver was
highly prized.

Many soldiers, particularly Southerners, got good weapons by removing them from dead Union soldiers or POWs. The South had a few armories, but for the most part, their weapon production was far behind the Union's. The C.S.A. managed to smuggle rifles from England, but blockade runners had a difficult time getting though Union barricades.

At Ft. Sumter, 4,000 Confederate shots were fired in only thirty-four hours of artillery exchange. Amazingly, no one died in the line of fire! The only casualty was accidental. Major Anderson wanted to salute the fallen U.S. flag, which had been shot down twice. During this ceremony, a burning ember struck a stack of cartridges, and young gunner Daniel Hough was killed in the resulting explosion.

In one of those bizarre twists of fate, Anderson had been Beauregard's artillery instructor at West Point; Anderson had been the dashing Creole's favorite instructor. Beauregard turned his guns on Anderson at Fort Sumter; evidently, the student had learned his lessons well.

BULL RUN BATTLEFIELD

"Quaker guns" were used frequently by the supply-deprived South; the C.S.A. improvised wherever it could. These "guns" were actually logs or other long pieces of wood which were used to create make-believe cannon. Most notably, Quaker guns were placed around Richmond's hills to keep the enemy guessing about how much fire-power the C.S.A. actually had.

THE NAVY:

The Navy did not make much of an appearance during the Civil War. The Confederate Navy was virtually non-existent, and what little Navy the United States had was widely scattered or in a sad state of disrepair. The function of the Navy during the War was twofold: (1) guard the Atlantic Coast against blockade runners and (2) squelch Confederate activity in the Gulf of Mexico (where Farragut uttered his immortal words, "Damn the torpedoes, full speed ahead!" as he laid waste to Mobile Bay).

To remedy the shortage of viable Navy warships, Lincoln did some fancy footwork. He told Secretary of War Gideon Welles to develop warships in a hurry to tide the Union over until the Navy could get up to speed. The result was the building of 90-day gunboats (built in less than three months), and "double-enders". Double-enders were kind of interesting because they had rudders at both ends, and were configured so they could turn at either end, without making time-consuming turns under enemy fire.

The Confederates got the bright idea of building an ironclad warship. They confiscated an almost-ruined wooden vessel left when Lincoln ordered Union ships at Norfolk destroyed at the beginning of the War. The C.S.A. carted the Merrimack away and tinkered with her until they had an ironclad, which they re-christened "the Virginia". Pleased as punch with their invention, they sashayed into Hampton Roads on March 8, 1862. Full of herself, Virginia shot hell out of two Union warships, sinking the Cumberland.

Upon hearing of the Virginia's assault, Secretary Welles ordered that barges be filled with stone. These barges would be made ready to sink in the Potomac River, in a bid to impede the Virginia's progress toward Washington, D.C. The Virginia was to destroy Washington, then sally forth to New York City and burn that city.

The next morning, the Virginia returned to Hampton Roads and bombarded the half-sunken warship Congress with hotshot. Just then, the **Union's** first ironclad, the Monitor, steamed into Hampton Roads and saw the mortally wounded Congress on fire. She faced the Virginia there at the mouth of Chesapeake Bay, and the steely ladies fired at each other for three hours. The battle was a draw, but the first ironclad battle effectively ended the use of wooden warships.

The South might not have had much of a Navy, but it **did** have the first submarine of modern design, the H.L. Hunley. The twenty-five foot Hunley sank four times with crews aboard during trial runs, but finally managed to torpedo and sink the U.S.S. Housatonic in Charleston Harbor.

BREADS

Not much actual bread making was done on the battlefield. There were few real bakers around, and adequate baking supplies and equipment were scarce. Small breads -- biscuits, cornbreads -- usually helped fill empty stomachs.

BISCUITS

Biscuits were served for breakfast, lunch or dinner. They could be eaten plain, with gravy over them, or as a sandwich with an often-coveted slice of ham, beef, sausage or fowl.

2 C flour
1½ tsp cream of tartar
1½ tsp baking soda
1/2 tsp salt
4 tbs lard
2/3 C milk or buttermilk (depends on personal tastes)

Heat oven to 400o. Mix dry ingredients, and cut in lard a bit at a time until mixture reaches the consistency of oatmeal. Stir in milk to make a dough. Sprinkle some flour over a flat surface and roll (or pat with hands) the dough into a 1/2 inch thickness. Use a coffee mug to punch out biscuits. Use as much of the dough as possible, putting scraps together and re-rolling until dough is used up. Bake 10-12 minutes (until biscuits are lightly browned).

FOR DROP BISCUITS: Prepare biscuits the same way as the recipe above, but instead of rolling dough out and cutting biscuits, drop desired-sized bits of batter onto baking surface. Bake 10-12 minutes (until lightly browned).

CORNBREAD

4 C cornmeal
2 tsp baking soda
2 tsp salt
4 eggs, beaten
4 C buttermilk or milk
1/2 C lard or bacon
    drippings

Heat Dutch oven to
425o. Combine dry ingre-
dients; make a well in the
center. Combine wet ingredients, mix well. Pour wet
mixture into well; blend.
Pour batter into whatever
pan is being used for baking,
and set the pan in the Dutch
oven.

Some folks bake cornbread
in a cast iron skillet, and
this is a fine idea if the skillet can be placed in an oven or
if someone can bake cornbread
over a fire. Bake 35-45 minutes
(until knife inserted in center
comes out clean and top of cornbread is golden brown).

CRACKLIN' BREAD

Cracklins' are small pieces of pork fat that have been fried until all the grease has been extracted. They give a nice flavor to cornbread, especially if meat is scarce and a small taste of meat is better than nothing at all.

1/4 C lard or bacon drippings
2 C cornmeal
2 tsp baking soda
1 tsp salt
2 eggs, beaten
2 C buttermilk or milk
1 C cracklins'

Put the lard or drippings in a baking pan and heat the Dutch oven to about 425o-450o. Combine cornmeal, baking soda, and salt; mix well. Combine the eggs and buttermilk and add to dry mixture; blend well. Stir in cracklins', mix well; put baking pan in the Dutch oven and bake for 25-30 minutes (until golden brown).

DUMPLINGS

Dumplings were used in a number of ways; they could be eaten alone as a side dish, they could be put in soups or they could be thrown into the pot with chicken.

4 C flour
1 tsp baking soda
1 tsp salt
6 tsp lard
1½ C buttermilk (or milk)

Combine the flour and baking soda, add salt. Cut in lard until mixture is like coarse meal. Add milk slowly, blend well with the dry mixture. Turn the dough out onto a floured surface and knead gently four or five times. Pat dough to a ¼" thickness, then pinch off 1½" inch pieces. Drop pieces into boiling water and boil 8-10 minutes, stirring once in a while.

GRIDDLE CAKES

Griddle cakes are
cornmeal pancakes.

1½ C cornmeal
½ C flour
2 tsp sugar
¼ tsp baking soda
¼ tsp cream of tartar
½ tsp salt
3/4 C buttermilk
½ C water
2 eggs, beaten
¼ C butter, melted

In a bowl, mix
dry ingredients.
Add buttermilk and
water, stir. Add
eggs, continue to
stir. Add butter,
stir well. Ladle
batter in 3 or 4
inch ovals into a
hot greased skillet.
Cook until brown,
1 to 2 minutes on
each side. Serve
hot, topped with
butter and fresh
berries or peaches.
Molasses is also a
good topping.

HARDTACK

Hardtack was rationed to both armies, and it was also made on the battlefield. It was simply made and gave soldiers and sailors something on which to chew. Since it was often harder than nails, troops might have to dunk it in hot coffee or soup to make it more palatable. Hardtack sometimes went by other names: sea biscuits, ship biscuit, 'tack, ironplate biscuits and army bread.

The beauty of hardtack was that it could be kept for long periods of time, although it often became insect infested -- an unpleasant surprise when boxes were opened in the field. It had to be kept very dry, otherwise it would quickly rot and/or get bugs.

The name "hardtack" came about because "hard" was the consistency of the biscuit, and "tack" was an English word meaning "food". Hardtack was given to English sailors years before the Civil War.

Recipe:
Flour
Water
Salt

Mix ingredients into an elastic dough. The dough must **not** be sticky. Roll or pat dough into a one-half inch thickness, then cut into 3 by 3 inch pieces. Use a nail or anything else with a sharp point to punch holes in the hardtack at regular intervals, making sure that the holes go all the way through; bake at 400o for about 20 minutes or until lightly browned.

HOE CAKES

These corn cakes got their name because slaves supposedly cooked them on their hoes in the hot sun.

1 C corn meal
1/2 tsp salt
1 tsp baking soda
1 tsp cream of tartar
2 tbs bacon drippings or lard
1/2 C milk or water

Mix dry ingredients; stir in bacon drippings and milk or water. Grease a heavy skillet with lard. Drop batter into skillet, shaping into four hoe cakes at a time. Brown on both sides.

JOHNNY CAKES

Also called "journey cakes," these corn cakes were carried by soldiers on their war journeys.

2 C flour
1½ tsp baking soda
1½ tsp cream of tartar
2 tbs butter
1 tsp salt
1/2 C water
lard

Mix dry ingredients; cut butter into mixture until completely blended. Add water a little at a time and knead until an elastic dough is formed; dough must not be sticky. Heat lard in a skillet over medium heat; form dough into slightly flattened 2-inch cakes. Fry the cakes, turning frequently, until all sides are golden brown.

PANCAKES

4 C flour
4 tbs sugar
½ tsp baking soda
½ tsp cream of tartar
½ tsp salt
1½ C milk (not
    buttermilk)
1 C water
4 eggs, beaten
½ C butter, melted

   In a bowl, mix
dry ingredients.
Add milk and water,
stir. Add eggs, stir.
Add butter, stir well.
Ladle batter in 3 or
4 inch ovals into a hot
greased skillet. Cook
until brown, 1 to 2
minutes on each side.

SALLY LUNN

1½ tbs milk   1/3 C water
4½ tsp butter (not lard)   2 eggs
1 tsp salt   1 tsp sugar
2 C flour   3/4 tsp yeast

Soak yeast in lukewarm water. Beat eggs well;
heat the milk to just warm, then add it and melted
butter to the eggs. Add sugar, salt, yeast mixture
and flour. Mix well; pour into bowl and let mixture
double in size.

When dough has doubled in size, punch it once or
twice and put it in a Dutch oven. Let it rise
1½ hours. Bake at 350o for 25 minutes (until
lightly browned).

BATTLEFIELD COOKING

Things took a bad turn for the C.S.A. after war was declared and the Union stopped shipping food and supplies to the South. Whatever food the South **did** produce could not be quickly or easily shipped because Southern railroads were inefficient. Food and supplies had to be unloaded at each southern state line. Goods were then reloaded onto another train. This time-consuming process was necessary because train tracks of most southern states were of different widths.

The North had machines to harvest crops faster; they also had ice to keep food fresh during shipment. The Union made use of dry or "dessicated" vegetables, and canned milk, vegetables and juice.

For daily rations, Yankees received a piece of meat, a loaf of bread, butter, dried beans, rice or hominy, coffee or tea, sugar or molasses, salt and pepper. Rebels got a small piece of meat irregularly and cornbread or hardtack.

Out of necessity, rebs were resourceful at finding food, but their renowned cleverness failed them as war ground on and livestock and vegetables grew scarcer and scarcer. Southerners had been generous with their

soldiers, freely offering them food. Civilians were eventually forced to stop feeding soldiers as encroaching Yankees depleted farms and plantations.

The lush and fertile Shenandoah Valley ("shenandoah" means "daughter of the stars" in the language of Native Americans who were the first inhabitants of the region) was known during the War as "The Breadbasket of the South" because it supplied many of the C.S.A.'s food needs.   The

Fisher's Hill Battlefield, Virginia
"The Gibraltar of the South"

gentle Valley (home to both sides of the author's family for two hundred and fifty years) was no longer productive after total warfare reared its merciless head throughout the area.

Fresh fruits, vegetables and dairy products were not available at any time as rations for either army. The powers that were on both sides felt that soldiers could use some ingenuity in locating certain food items. These items could usually be purchased from Union sutlers who followed Union camps and set up a type of tented general store, or they might be bought or "appropriated" from locals.

Just about everything was fried in lard,
especially in the South. Some war scholars postu-
late that the high fat diet was a contributing factor
in the South's loss: Soldiers spent much of their
time in the latrine, often missing calls to action.

LARD

Cut fresh, uncured pork fat into
cubes; wash in cold water. Press
out washing water and cut fat
into smaller cubes. Put cubes in
large kettle, bring to a good
simmer until water evaporates
and fat begins to melt. Reduce
heat to low, and cook until fat
is totally rendered (separated)
from all solid tissue. Check pot
often; do not let fat burn. Lard
is ready when solid tissue sinks
to bottom and starts to brown
(these pieces are cracklins').
Allow cracklins' to get crisp.
Remove kettle from fire, and
remove cracklins'. Cool lard;
don't let it start to harden.
Pour into metal containers;
store in a cool, dark place.

MEATS:

Meats were consumed fresh, or could be
preserved by salting, smoking or drying.

HOW TO SALT MEAT

Meat can be salted either by soaking
it in salt water (brine), or by covering it with
salt. Salt acts as a preservative by deactivating
bacteria; it does **not** cook meat.

THE SALTING PROCESS

Lay a 1½" layer of salt in a
barrel. Pack a layer of meat
as tightly as possible in the
barrel. Cover meat with 1½" of
salt, pack in another tight layer
of meat, cover with another 1½"
of salt, keep repeating layers.

Make a salty brine and pour it
over meat, being **sure** to weight
meat down. Cover meat with a
couple of inches of brine, and
leave it alone for a couple of
weeks.

SMOKING MEAT

To smoke meat, all that needed to be done
was to put meat over a smokey fire and cook it until
it was done; meat was cooked at a low temperature.
It was better to put the smoking meat in a tent, a
a cave or in some other closed-in area if possible.

DRYING MEAT

Meat is hung in dry air after being lightly
salted. As in the process of smoking meat, meat is
best dried in a closed-in place.

THE COOKS:

Some units had an official cook while others
were a communal affair with many soldiers pitching in.
Cooks were among the smartest fellows in camp, because
they were able to stretch food and come up with
different ways of preparing the same ingredients. No
matter who did the cooking, beggars could not be
choosers. Each man was expected to eat whatever was
put in front of him or go hungry. This **was** war, after

all! Any heroic or romantic illusions soldiers
entertained about any aspect of war were quickly
dashed; men hardly out of boyhood grew up fast.

Coffee, a much
desired item, was **very**
scarce in the South, but
the North seemed to have
plenty of coffee beans.
A concoction of fake
coffee could be made by
by drying acorns, removing the shells, roasting, and
then grinding or finely crushing the nut meat, but
most soldiers preferred real coffee. The substitute
was choked down as a last resort. Often, when the two
sides met under non-combat conditions, Confederate
tobacco was exchanged for Union coffee beans. Tobacco
was also bartered for much needed Union medicines or
whiskey.

Whiskey and beer, like coffee, were often
haphazard concoctions, made with questionable ingredients under less than optimum conditions. Even
vile whiskey and beer served the purpose, helping
soldiers to relieve boredom and the stress of war.

COOKING EQUIPMENT:

When camp was set up, a small pit was dug and filled with coal or wood. A gridiron was set over

the coals or the wood. This gridiron held pots, pans, coffee pots, skillets, or the ubiquitous Dutch oven:

Dutch ovens were the true stars of **any** camp -- the undisputed champs! They were versatile and indispensable. Temperatures in a Dutch oven were regulated by how hot coals in the pit were or by how high flames from the wood fire were. Dutch ovens were used to roast, bake, fry, simmer, or to make stews or soups. Cooks could get along without just about any other type of cooking equipment, but they could not do without their Dutch oven.

Kettles were also used often. Their uses ranged from making soups or stews and cooking vegetables to washing clothes. Not many clothes (or people) got washed on the battle-field (most soldiers had lice), but it was good to know the means were available.

Kettles were suspended from an ell-shaped bar or placed on the gridiron. Hot coals or a wood fire were needed for simmering or boiling, and the hotter the coals or higher the flames, the hotter the temperature would be.

Cast iron skillets were another camp necessity. Meat could be fried, gravies or hash

could be made, and potatoes or other vegetables could be fried. Sometimes, fried vegetables and cornbread or biscuits were all the dinner that was to be had. Some fellows developed the wonderful and envied knack of baking cornbread in a skillet. Skillet-baked cornbread is a treat not to be missed!

"SEASONING" CAST IRON SKILLETS:

Cast iron skillets have to be "seasoned" before being used. When first bought, they are pewter gray. To season a cast iron skillet, it was first washed with soap and water and **thoroughly** dried. To keep the iron from rusting, a thin coat of lard (nowadays, vegetable oil could be used) was spread **all over** the skillet.

After greasing, the skillet was placed in a 300o Dutch oven for 15 minutes (if it would not fit into a Dutch oven, it was placed on a gridiron and covered with a large lid). When it had cooled, excess interior grease was wiped to evenly coat the surface. Return skillet to oven and bake 1½ hours. After the skillet cooled to room temperature, the entire process was repeated a couple of more times.

A SOLDIER'S LIFE

Who **were** the men who fought this long and bloody war, and what were their lives like? The U.S. Army said that soldiers had to be eighteen years old in order to be issued a rifle, but younger boys could be given swords. The Confederate Army pretty much armed any healthy male between the ages of sixteen and sixty.

Both sides had little boys serving -- about 60,000 small boys answered the call to arms. Some were buglers or powder monkeys on warships, but most were drummers.

The most famous drummer boy was Johnny Clem, who started hanging around the U.S. Army at the tender age of nine. At first, he was a mild amusement and mascot to his older comrades; their attitude toward him was that of big brothers. Ask older brothers why they pick on younger brothers and they will reply, "Because they're there, and it's just so easy."

The mens' gentle teasing soon turned to admiration as Johnny became a minor celebrity. He proved his mettle at Shiloh, and newspapers took to calling him "Johnny Shiloh." He killed at least one rebel at Chickamauga; the rebel hollered for Johnny to "come and get him," and Johnny was only too happy to oblige.

A few years later, Johnny got a bee in his bonnet to enroll at West Point. West Point did not want him because he had a third-grade education. He whined, and Grant took pity on him, making him a second lieutenant. Johnny spent fifty-five years in the Army, retiring as a major general.

Most soldiers were farm boys or small town boys in their late teens or early twenties. Southern boys had two reasons for fighting: a belief in the ideals of the Confederate States of America, and a chance to escape the stifling boredom of farms. Northern young men wanted to broaden their horizons and many got caught up in the romance of going off to war. Soldiers on neither side fully realized the horrors that awaited them.

UNIFORMS:

Uniforms for all soldiers were expensive and hard to come by. Soldiers were expected to take good care of their uniforms. The U.S. Army was usually well supplied, and their uniforms were of decent quality. The U.S. Army was adamant about soldiers' uniforms being standardized.

The Union had plenty of factories for the production of uniforms, and getting material was not a real problem. The North knew it could get material from Europe, since relations with the cotton-producing South were strained.

The C.S.A. had a harder time supplying uniforms. The South had cotton, but having enough

factories to make uniforms was another matter. There was a large factory in Richmond, and many soldiers wore what was called a Richmond Depot jacket made of a cheap "butternut" dye concocted of oak, logwood and sumac. This dye produced a gray cloth that turned tan in the sun and weather. Uniform pants were made from the same cloth. C.S.A. enlisted soldiers sometimes wore inexpensive "sack coats," cheaply made from easily obtained, loosely woven fabric.

51

As the War dragged on, rebels wore whatever they could find, often stripping dead soldiers, then trading around camp to find a uniform or parts of a uniform that would fit. Some fellows were downright enterprising, like the rebel who grabbed up eleven hats from fallen comrades after the Battle of Cedar Creek. He figured he could perhaps sell the hats as souvenirs after the War. When rebels got hold of Union uniforms, they often dyed the uniforms with butternut dye.

On some occasions, rebels wore civilian clothes. Wearing civilian clothes for battle never bothered the 3,500 Native Americans who fought for the South. They always wore their own attire, figuring everyone would know on whose side they were fighting.

In a perfect world, the administrations of both armies laid out lists for what soldiers would receive. Of course, no perfect world existed in this war and the lists were a source of dour amusement among troops. The lists optimistically designated for each soldier: two jackets the first year, one each for the following two years, one overcoat, cap, socks (twelve pair), drawers (seven).

Even if the designated clothing **was** available for all Union and Confederate troops (which it was not) allowances were woefully insufficient for the rigorous demands of soldiering. Some soldiers wrote home for needed clothing, others took from the dead, and others did without. Wool for winter uniforms and blankets was hard to come by for both sides, but there was plenty of cotton for shirts and underwear. Overcoats were almost nonexistent.

A soldier's pay did not go far. Union privates received $13 a month and a clothing allowance of $42 a year. A Confederate private received $11 a month until near the end of the war when he received a raise to $18 a month to help compensate for inflation.

SOLDIERING EQUIPMENT:

The question would then arise that if blankets and overcoats were very scarce, how did soldiers manage to keep warm in the winter? To

partially settle the blanket problem, blankets were
often made of a cotton-wool blend and some were made
of rubber. Soldiers had waterproofed rubber ponchos
to keep rain and snow at a distance.

Southern soldiers did not carry tents
because tents were too heavy. Sleeping conditions
often left much to be desired. Rebels, country boys
that they were, bivouacked in the woods, sleeping on
canvas or rubber ground covers. They "spooned" on
cold nights, relying on body heat to keep warm. When
it rained or snowed, they slept two together and put
one poncho on the ground and one on top.

Yankees did use tents, because they often
had wagons to carry large wall tents and could throw
their tents on the wagons. Tents soldiers used were
called "dog tents" because these small tents were

barely large enough for a dog. Each man carried half
a tent. When they got to camp, two men buttoned their
halves together, stretched them between poles or
upended rifles, and staked them to the ground.

Some things soldiers ideally carried were:
shoes (optimistic hope), a cartridge box, bayonet,
canteen, overcoat, blanket, socks, underwear, shirts,

handkerchief, haversack (tarred or painted black to waterproof it), a rifle or rifle musket, hardtack, pocket knife, comb, toothbrush, housewife (no, **not** the comely next-door neighbor from back home -- a "housewife" was a sewing kit), wallet, cup, plate, eating utensils, money, writing paper, and pen or pencil.

Not all soldiers had access to all these items; some men, preferring to travel light, ditched items. Others never had access to coveted personal items. Things got so bad towards the end that men sometimes received letters from home written on wallpaper.

At first, soldiers carried knapsacks, as proud as peacocks of this handsome addition to their uniforms. Their pride turned to dismay because knapsacks weighed fifty pounds or more when fully loaded. A daily fifteen-mile march was not unheard of, and the men complained that the cumbersome straps cut into their backs, shoulders, arms and chests. This was long before the days of lightweight, modern knapsacks designed for maximum comfort.

Many soldiers discarded the hated knapsacks and went instead to using blanket-rolls. To make a blanket-roll, belongings were rolled into a blanket, then tied on both ends. The roll was slung over a shoulder. The Union Army developed lighter knapsacks towards the end of the War, but soldiers were skeptical of using the new inventions. Memories of the hated old-fashioned knapsacks died hard.

DIVERSIONS:

For all the camp and battlefield hardships suffered by both sides, there **were** some pleasant diversions. Men played cards, told stories, wrote letters, kept their journals up-to-date, ran races, had ball games, wagered bets, played checkers and chess, and whittled.

They also played musical instruments, and once in a while it happened that each side, in an atmosphere of non-combativeness, visited each other's camps for impromptu jam sessions. Music from bugles, fiddles, harmonicas and banjos rang out sweet and clear, entertaining everyone in camp. At these times, soldiers could forget hostilities for a while and be their lively young selves.

Soldiers sang to their music and, if whiskey was available as it often was, one can imagine that a bit of merry dancing and high stepping went on. The specter of war loomed like a great bloodthirsty beast with claws and fangs that overshadowed the mens' days and nights, but the fighting fellows made the best of things.

MEAT, POULTRY AND SEAFOOD

ALLIGATOR

It is imperative that people refer to
the description of how gators were (and still
are) killed before trying this recipe at home.
In fact, trying this recipe **could** lead to having
neighbors call the funny-farm wagon (for the
aspiring cook, not for the gator) especially if
the now-angry critter gets loose and starts a
neighborhood rampage while merely trying to find
his way back to peaceful hearth and kin.

This advice of reading the gator-killing
technique **especially** applies to Yankees, who have
probably never encountered a wild gator in their
lives (the well-fed gators you saw with the family
at Gatorland while in Orlando on summer vacation do
not count!).

Recipe:
Meat from gator's tail, legs and sides
1 C flour
salt and pepper
2 eggs, beaten
½ C lard

Cut gator meat into bite-sized pieces. Mix flour,
salt and pepper. Dip gator meat into eggs, then
into flour mixture. Heat lard and fry meat until
lightly browned.

ARTIFICIAL OYSTERS

Although real oysters were plentiful
during the War, sometimes they were not always
available when the fellows got a hankering for
them. "Artificial oysters" tasted almost like
the real thing, and satisfied cravings.

1 C flour
1 tsp sugar
1 tsp salt
pepper
2 eggs, beaten
3 ears of fresh corn cut from the cob
  (retain milky juice when corn is cut)
½ C milk
2 tbs lard

Combine flour, sugar, salt and pepper in a bowl;
mix. In another bowl, combine eggs, corn, milk
and 2 tbs lard or butter. Stir the corn mixture
into dry ingredients. Shape the mixture into
patties and fry in heated lard until golden,
turning patties once.

BARBEQUE

Barbeque, during the time of the Civil War, referred to a method of very slowly cooking meat, **not** to the sauce which was used to baste the meat. The basting sauce used was incidental to the actual act of barbequing. Sauces using a tomato (ketsup) base are a modern invention; in the time of the War, basting sauces did not use a tomato base. Nowadays, much ado is made of fancy and exotic barbeque sauces; in the War days, the meat and the method of cooking it were the stars of the show.

Proper barbequing was a lively and jovial affair that took all night (or all day) with many people pitching in. It was not something through which people could rush. Pork or beef meat (pork was preferred) was put on a spit over a smokey fire or else a large pit was dug and the meat was put on a gridiron about a foot over the pit and slowly smoke-cooked. The meat was basted from time to time with a light sauce, then when done, was pulled from the bones and coarsely chopped.

SAUCE:

Butter
salt and pepper
vinegar (if available)

Mix as much sauce as needed (depends on the amount of meat), and salt and pepper to taste. Baste the cooking meat from time to time. Cook meat until it is very, very tender.

BAKED CHICKEN

1 chicken
salt and pepper
butter

Wash chicken and remove innards. Place chicken,
top side up in a Dutch oven. Sprinkle salt and
pepper over chicken and brush with butter. Bake,
uncovered, at 350o for 45-60 minutes (until chicken
is an even golden brown). Baste chicken with
butter from time to time while it is baking.

BEEF LIVER

1 beef liver, thinly sliced
$\frac{1}{4}$ C flour
salt and pepper
2 tbs lard
For the gravy:
1 onion, chopped (if available)
3 tbs lard
$1\frac{1}{2}$ C water
1 tbs flour
salt and pepper

Combine flour, salt and pepper. Coat liver in flour
mixture, then brown in 2 tbs lard. Remove liver from
pan.
To make the gravy:
Saute onion in 3 tbs lard, add flour, stir often
until the roux (flour and lard) is the color of a
penny. Gradually add water, stirring constantly
until smooth. Add salt and pepper, pour gravy over
liver. Bake at 350o for 40-50 minutes (until liver
is tender).

CHICKEN AND DUMPLINGS

The recipe for dumplings
is in the Breads section.

1 chicken, skinned and cut
   up
water
salt and pepper

Put chicken in Dutch oven;
add water and salt. Bring
to a boil, cover, reduce
heat; simmer one hour
(until tender). Remove
chicken and let it cool
enough to be able to pull
the meat off. Cut meat
into bite-sized pieces; set
aside.

Add dumplings to boiling
water, reduce heat to medium;
cook 8-10 minutes, stirring
from time to time.

CHICKEN FRICASSEE

Chicken fricassee was said to be a personal favorite of Thomas Jefferson. Civil War cooks often prepared it as a "special occasion" meal. It took a bit of extra work and attention to prepare, but the result was worth the effort.

3 C boiling water
2 good-sized chickens, cut up and skinned
salt and pepper
1 bay leaf (if available)
mushrooms (if available)
1½ tbs flour
3 onions, chopped
2 egg yolks

Combine boiling water, chicken, bay leaf, salt and pepper in a Dutch oven. Cover and let stand for 10 or 15 minutes. Remove the chicken and bay leaf. Add 3 tbs water to Dutch oven, slowly add flour, stirring to thoroughly blend. Add chicken and reserved liquid. Cover and simmer for 30 minutes, then add onion to mixture. Cover and simmer another 30 minutes.

Remove chicken and place it where it can be kept warm. Pour a little bit of the hot broth mixture into the egg yolks and add yolks to the remaining broth mixture, stirring all the while. Cook over a low heat for 3 minutes (until thickened), then pour sauce over chicken. Serve immediately.

CHICKEN LIVERS

1 C flour
salt and pepper
2 pounds chicken
   livers, cut in
   half
lard

Combine flour, salt
and pepper. Dredge
livers in flour; fry
in hot lard until
brown (3-5 minutes).
Serve livers over
hot rice or noodles.

CHICKEN POT PIE

1 good-sized chicken (or turkey), cut up
3 or 4 potatoes, peeled and diced
3 or 4 carrots, chopped
2 onions, chopped
2 or 3 celery stalks (if available), chopped
3-3/4 C flour
1 tsp salt
pepper
1¼ C lard
8 to 10 tbs cold water
¼ C butter
½ C flour

Cook chicken in boiling water (just enough to cover chicken) 45-60 minutes (until tender); drain and reserve broth. Pull meat from bones, cut into bite-sized pieces; set aside. Cook vegetables in broth 20-25 minutes; drain and keep broth.

To make crust: Combine flour and salt; cut in lard until mixture looks like coarse meal; stir in water, a tablespoon at a time, to moisten dry ingredients. Shape dough into a ball; remove two-thirds. Cover and keep remaining dough cool (cold is even better).

Roll (or pat) dough into a rectangle large enough to fit in Dutch oven (if you don't have a Dutch oven, any large roasting pan or covered casserole will be fine). Melt butter over low heat; add ½ C flour, stir until smooth. Cook 1 minute, stir all the while. Slowly add broth, cook over medium heat (stir constantly) until broth is thickened. Stir in salt, pepper, chicken and vegetables and pour into pastry-lined dish.

Roll (or pat) remaining dough into a rectangle and place on top of chicken potpie; fold edges under. Cut slits in the top to allow steam to escape. Brush top of crust with melted butter. Bake at 400o 35-40 minutes (until crust is a light golden brown).

DOVES

It takes quite a few doves to make a recipe stretch very far. With this in mind, if you have only a few doves with which to work, other items (potatoes, other vegetables, cornbread or biscuits) take up the slack. During the War, no meat or game could be allowed to go to waste.

1 C flour
salt and pepper
10-12 doves, cleaned
½ C butter or lard (butter would be better)
1 onion, chopped (if available)

Combine flour, salt and pepper and dredge doves in flour. Brown the doves and onions in butter in a skillet. Cover and cook over a low heat 20-30 minutes (until tender).

DUCK

Nowadays, duck is something of a ritzy delicacy. Back in the days of the War, duck was simply... duck.

1 good-sized duck, cleaned and dressed
salt and pepper

Remove giblets and neck from duck. Sprinkle the cavity with salt and pepper, and prick the skin with a fork at two-inch intervals. Put duck, breast side up, in a Dutch oven and bake, uncovered, at 350o for 2-2½ hours (until tender). Since duck is greasy to begin with, basting with butter is not necessary.

EEL

Eels - however many
   you have
2 eggs, beaten
salt and pepper
cornmeal
lard or butter

Skin and clean eel(s),
cut into bite-sized
pieces; sprinkle with
salt and leave for an
hour or so. Rinse and
dry eels, dip in egg,
then in cornmeal; fry
them up in lard.

FRIED CHICKEN

There were (and are) two types of fried
chicken: regular and batter-dipped (crispy). There
are important things to know about frying chicken
before getting to the point of putting it on the
table. These things help separate the fried chicken
experts from the hopefuls.

First off, a cast iron skillet is the **only**
way to fry. If someone wants to deep-fry rather
than pan fry, a deeper pot or pan is used. For
deep-frying, the pot or pan must be filled no more
than halfway with lard (lard must come halfway up
the sides of chicken pieces). If too much lard is
used, very greasy chicken will be the result; hardly
any food is worse than greasy chicken.

The frying fat: Clean fat must **always** be
used, and must be kept hot while frying chicken. The
temperature drops when chicken is added, then it goes
up again. Always remember that the fat is very hot
and should never be left unattended. Be aware that

65

hot fat can "spritz" on arms, hands or faces. Be
gentle with the chicken as it is moved around during
cooking -- you want the fat to splash as little as
possible.

TIP: Bacon drippings (not too many!) can be added
to the fat for an interesting flavor.

FRIED CHICKEN, BATTER-FRIED
(CRISPY)

1½ C buttermilk
salt
pepper (if a hotter chicken is desired, use more
    pepper, but be sure not to overdo the pepper --
    some **don't** like it hot!)
2 chickens cut up
2 C flour
lard

Combine buttermilk, salt and pepper, stir well.
Place the chicken in a container and pour the
buttermilk mixture over it. Cover and let chicken
stand for 20 minutes, turning once. Remove chicken.

Dredge the chicken in flour, making sure to coat
the chicken well. Cook in lard (about 350o) until
the chicken is browned on both sides (turning only
once). Reduce heat to about 275o, cover and cook 25
minutes. If you like, you can set a shallow pan
under a mostly clean gridiron and put the chicken
on the gridiron so that grease drips into the pan.

FRIED CHICKEN
(REGULAR)

2 chickens, cut up
1 tsp salt
pepper
4 C flour
1 egg, beaten
1 C milk

Season chicken with salt and pepper. Add flour;
set aside. Combine egg and milk; dip chicken in
egg mixture, then dredge in flour mixture, making
sure to coat the chicken well.

Heat about one inch of lard in a skillet to a
temperature of 350o and place chicken in skillet.

Cover, and cook chicken over medium heat for 20-25
minutes (until golden brown). Chicken can be
drained of fat.

GRAVY FOR FRIED CHICKEN

Pour all but 3 tablespoons of
lard from skillet, but leave all
the browned pieces in the skillet.
Put skillet back on a medium heat.
Add 2 tablespoons of flour to the
fat, and stir the flour into the
lard; stir constantly until it
turns brown. Gradually add 2 C
milk (if there is not enough milk,
1 C water can be substituted, but
it is much better to use all milk).
Keep stirring **constantly**; gravy
will thicken, and is finished when
it reaches the desired consistency.
Salt and pepper to taste.

FRIED FISH

Fish (however many and whatever kind you have),
   cleaned
salt and pepper
cornmeal
lard

Combine cornmeal with salt and pepper, mix well.
Dredge fish in the cornmeal mixture until fish is
lightly coated, then fry the fish in the lard until
fish is golden brown. Drain fish well, because it
will be quite greasy.

FROG LEGS

No soldier was likely to get a full belly
from eating a mess of frog legs. Frog legs are
too small, and it would take too many to make a
really substantial meal for a lot of people. Six
small pairs of frog legs or three huge pairs will
feed one person; this translates to roughly one
pound per person. However, they **are** meat and
protein, and a filling meal could be made by serving
them with cornbread and potatoes. Much of the fun of
bringing frog legs back to camp would be in catching
the little fellows.

Recipe:
Frog legs (as many as you have)
eggs, beaten (one egg per pound of frog legs)
salt and pepper
3/4 - 1 C milk
1 tbs lard
flour

Wash frog legs and place in a Dutch oven. Combine
milk, eggs, lard and salt; mix well. Sprinkle frog
legs with salt and pepper, dip in batter, dredge well
in flour. Fry until brown in hot lard; drain.

GOOSE

1 goose, dressed
salt and pepper

Remove giblets and neck; rinse goose, pat dry. Prick skin at 3-inch intervals. Place goose, breast side up, in Dutch oven. Bake, uncovered, at 350o 2-2½ hours (until meat is tender).

HASH

Beef-- however much you have (hash is a good way
    to use up leftover scraps of beef) -- chopped
8 C cooked potato, finely chopped
2 onions, chopped
salt and pepper
lard or butter

Heat lard in a skillet; add potatoes, meat, onion and seasonings. Spread evenly in skillet; cook over a medium heat for 10 minutes (until bottom is browned), stirring from time to time.

MEAT LOAF

Meat loaf was a way to use a little bit of meat to feed a lot of people. Civil War meat loaf was a mishmash of whatever ingredients were on hand.

beef and/or pork, chopped fine (remove most
    of the fat)
breadcrumbs from biscuits or cornbread --
    enough to bind meat(s) together
1 egg, beaten
2 onions, chopped
2 green peppers, chopped (if available)
1 or 2 tomatoes (if available)
salt and pepper

Peel and cook tomatoes into a sauce consistency. Mix meat, breadcrumbs, egg, onion, green pepper, salt and pepper together; blend well. Stir the tomato sauce into the meat mixture. Form meat mixture into a loaf in a Dutch oven, and bake at 350o for one hour.

MUTTON

Cut fat off the mutton and roast in a Dutch oven at a medium heat (350o) for 2-2½ hours.

Another way to roast mutton was to roast it over a spit until done, 1½-2 hours, turning it from time to time.

MUTTON WITH VEGETABLES

2 lbs mutton meat
2 turnips or parsnips, chopped (if available)
2 or 3 celery stalks, chopped (if available)
1 onion, chopped
2 tomatoes, unpeeled and coarsely chopped
2 or 3 carrots, chopped
a couple of potatoes, peeled and cut up
salt and pepper
flour
lard

Cut mutton into bite-sized pieces and cut off all
fat. Heat lard in a skillet, dredge mutton in
flour and fry until brown. Remove meat and cook
vegetables in skillet with water to cover for
15-20 minutes (until potatoes are done). Return
mutton to skillet, season it, and simmer everything
for 1½ hours.

OYSTERS

Oysters were very plentiful during the War,
and were not considered delicacies as they are
today. Abraham Lincoln held huge oyster dinners,
having oysters packed in ice and rushed to his home
in Illinois. He continued to host oyster parties
once he got to Washington, D.C., where he was much
closer to the source of his culinary delight.

Oysters (as many as were available)
1 egg, beaten
salt
cornmeal
lard

Pat oysters dry; dip oysters in egg, shake gently to
remove some of egg mixture; immediately dredge
oysters in cornmeal. Fry oysters in hot lard for a
minute or two (until golden brown).

PORK ROAST

To roast pork, meat from the shoulders or the loins would be taken. It was important to roast pork well to prevent parasites from being consumed -- no traces of pink should remain in the meat. Overcooking would result in a tough, dry roast, so the meat had to be watched carefully. As the lesser of two evils, however, meat that was too well done was preferable to underdone meat.

Most of the fat should be trimmed away, but the meat should be roasted with the fat side up; as the meat roasts, the fat melts a bit, acting as a self-baster.

Pork should be roasted in a Dutch oven at a temperature of 325o, and 30 minutes of roasting time is allowed per pound.

PORK AND PARSNIPS

Fry up some pork (leftover meat is good for this recipe). Boil a mess of parsnips, with a little salt added, for 20-25 minutes; drain. Stir pork into the hot parsnips, add a little butter.

POSSUM

Possum is nasty. For one thing, a possum is uglier than a mudpost. It's hard to imagine how a mama possum could love her scrawny, pink-eyed offspring. It's even **more** difficult to picture how a male and female possum could create babies in the first place (but if **rhinos** can look to the inner beauty and reproduce, supposedly any creatures can).

As further proof of the possum's general unattractiveness, when cooked up, they are very greasy. Most people will not willingly eat possum, but as in everything else in life, there are exceptions. Some good old boys consider themselves blessed if a possum fortuitously appears. Other gourmands actively search out the mangy varmints.

Pickier eaters like to "purge" a possum. Purging involves keeping the creature confined for two or three days and feeding it lettuce, grass or other greens. Since possums eat anything and everything, purging supposedly removes all garbage from their system. True he-men, however, do not need to utilize the sissified purging system.

On the battlefield, if people were hungry enough, they could probably choke possum down (especially if cookie claimed temporary amnesia as to the origin of the meat being served up).

Recipe:
1 possum, cleaned and gutted
salt and pepper

Put possum in a Dutch oven and bake at 350o for 30-40 minutes.

Or, possum can be spit-roasted over a medium fire until done (1-1½ hours).

QUAIL
(BOBWHITE)

Quail is delicate, and calls for careful treatment. It overcooks easily, so quick cooking is necessary to keep it from becoming inedible.

FRIED QUAIL:

Quail, dressed (as many as you have)
salt and pepper
flour
lard

Remove skin and innards from quail. Mix the flour, salt and pepper together; dredge quail in the flour mixture. Fry quail quickly in hot lard until lightly browned.

ROASTED QUAIL:

Quail, dressed (as many as you have)
salt and pepper

Remove innards, but keep skin on quail (quail are very dry and the skin will act as a self-baster during slow cooking). Put quail in a Dutch oven and roast at 350o for 15-25 minutes (until just tender -- do not overcook these birds).

POT ROAST

1 chuck roast
1 or 2 onions, sliced (if available)
salt and pepper

Put roast in a Dutch oven, season with salt and
pepper. Add water to oven; add onions to the
water. Simmer roast for about 2½ hours, making
sure the water level remains the same. Once in
a while, spoon onion water over the roast.

POT ROAST GRAVY

4 tbs broth
4 tbs flour
2 C broth from pot roast
salt and pepper

In a skillet, combine 4 tbs broth and the flour;
stir until smooth. Cook 1 minute, stirring all the
while. Slowly add 2 C broth and cook over medium
heat, stirring constantly, until gravy is thickened.
Stir in salt and pepper (if needed -- check to be
sure first, because the cooking broth is already
seasoned).

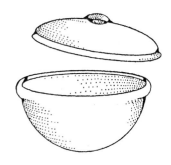

RABBIT (BAKED)

1 rabbit, cleaned and gutted
1 onion, chopped
2 C water
flour
salt and pepper
lard

Cut rabbit into four quarters and pat dry.
Combine flour, salt and pepper, mix well. Dredge
rabbit pieces in flour. Fry rabbit in hot lard
until light brown all over. Remove rabbit from
skillet; add onions to the lard and cook until
transparent (5-10 minutes). Add water to the
skillet and onions and return rabbit to skillet.

Simmer over a very low heat, covered, 1-1½ hours.

RABBIT (ROASTED)

1 rabbit, cleaned and skinned
salt and pepper

Tie rabbit to a spit over coals or a low-burning
fire. Roast rabbit for 1½-2 hours, turning the
spit often.

RACCOON

1 medium-sized raccoon, skinned and dressed
flour
salt and pepper

Wash coon and cut into bite-sized pieces. Mix
flour, salt and pepper and dredge coon pieces.
Brown meat in hot lard until lightly brown.
Bake in a 350o Dutch oven for 2-2½ hours.

RED BEANS AND RICE

dry red or kidney beans
1 C onion, chopped
salt and pepper
cooked rice

Pick over and wash beans, put into a large pot.
Add water and bring to a boil, reduce heat and
simmer for two minutes. Remove from heat and let
sit, covered, for one hour. **Or** you can pick over
and wash beans, cover with water and a lid and let
them sit overnight.

Drain beans, add onion and 3-5 cups of fresh
water. Bring to boil, reduce heat. Cover and
simmer 1½-2½ hours (until beans are tender). Add
water if necessary and stir from time to time.

During the last 15 or 20 minutes of cooking,
uncover beans and let them cook, allowing a thick
gravy to form. Serve over cooked rice.

ROAST BEEF

1 chuck, rump or round roast
salt and pepper

Wash and pat dry the roast. Secure it to a spit
and cook over a low-burning fire for 2-2½ hours,
turning the spit from time to time.

SAUSAGE

lean pork or beef
salt
pepper
sage (if available)

Chop meat into tiny
pieces -- as small
as possible. Mix meat
thoroughly with other
ingredients. Form
into patties, fry
well on both sides
(until browned).

SMITHFIELD HAM

Smithfield, Virginia is famous for its hams. Smithfield hams have been around since Colonial days, and the curing and aging process has remained the same since those early days. The curing and aging process is a big secret, and only hams cured within the Smithfield town limits can, by law, be called Smithfield hams.

When Northern troops passed through that area, they were aghast when they saw the hams. They thought they were moldy and had gone bad. They did not know what they were missing!

Recipe:

Soak a Smithfield ham for about 12 hours. The mold must then be scrubbed from the ham; the ham is put into a kettle with fresh water and simmered for 4-5 hours. Allow the ham to cool in its cooking water.

When it is cool enough to handle, peel off the skin and most of the fat. Put the ham fat side up (for self-basting) in a Dutch oven and cut a few slits on the top. Roast at 450o for 20-30 minutes (until browned).

FRIED HAM: Slices can be cut from the cooked ham and fried in lard. Fried ham makes a wonderful meal (sending most Southerners into fits of ectasy), particularly with the addition of cornbread, fried potatoes and greens. Fried ham can be made from **any** cooked ham, not just a Smithfield.

SQUABS

Squabs are immature pigeons, and they were plentiful during the 19th century. Some folks liked them, others did not. When asked if he would eat pigeon, one grizzled old Rebel replied, "If I ain't got nothin' else to eat."

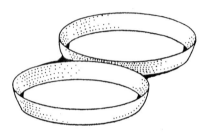

8 squabs, dressed
salt and pepper
water

Bake the squabs in a Dutch oven in a little bit of water at about 425o for 25 minutes.

SQUIRREL

It was a familiar sight to me during my childhood to see skinned and dressed squirrels hanging around waiting to be cooked. Now, as I feed and coddle squirrels (and watch them tear the deck and screens up), I find it hard to reconcile the childhood and the adult images. I keep saying I'm going to stop feeding them, but then one does a spectacular or endearing trick, and the peanuts and chocolate chips flow freely again. These squirrels really know their business.

I never ate squirrel as a child, but years later had a bite or two of squirrel stew in Florida, near the banks of the Suwanee River.

There's one certain thing about squirrels: there is a ton of them around. They were used often during the War because of their easy availability.

Recipe:

1 squirrel, skinned and dressed
salt and pepper
flour
lard

Cut squirrel into quarters. Combine flour, salt and pepper and dredge squirrel pieces in mixture. Fry in hot lard until nicely browned.

SQUIRREL FRICASSEE

8 squirrels, skinned and dressed
1 C flour
salt and pepper
8 C water
lard

Combine flour, salt and pepper; dredge squirrel in flour mixture. Brown squirrel in hot lard in a cast iron skillet. Add 2 C water and bring to a boil; reduce heat to low and simmer about one hour, adding water if necessary.

Combine 2 C water and a tablespoon of flour; stir well. Slowly add wet flour mixture to skillet, stirring all the while. Cook over low heat until thickened.

STEAK

beef steaks
salt and pepper
lard or butter

Heat lard in a skillet, and place steaks in the
pan; salt and pepper the steaks. Fry over a
medium to high heat until steaks are done, turning once during cooking.

TURKEY

1 turkey, dressed
salt
butter

Remove giblets and neck from turkey (save
for gravy). Wash turkey, pat dry and truss.

Put turkey in Dutch oven, breast side up; brush
entire bird with butter. Bake at 325o for 4-5
hours. Turkey is done when drumsticks can be
easily moved up and down.

GIBLET GRAVY: Chop giblets, neck and liver. Add
onion, celery, salt; cover with water and boil.
Cover, reduce heat, simmer 45 minutes. Drain,
reserve broth; set giblets aside.

Add broth to pan drippings (loosen sediment from
bottom of Dutch oven). Take 1½ C of broth mixture
(add water if necessary). Combine flour and ¼ C
water in a saucepan, stirring until smooth. Add
broth mixture and cook over medium heat, stir until
gravy is thickened. Stir in neck meat, giblets, a
beaten egg and pepper. Serve hot.

VENISON ROAST

I remember sitting around a fire watching
a venison roast being cooked on a spit. When the
meat was judged to be done, each person helped
themself.

1 venison roast
salt

Put the venison roast on a spit (tie it onto the
spit) and roast at 350o (over a medium-high fire)
for 2-2½ hours (until meat is done).

VENISON STEAK

venison steaks (with fat trimmed)
flour
salt and pepper
lard

Heat lard in a cast iron skillet; combine flour,
salt and pepper in a bowl, dredge venison steaks in
flour mixture, then fry steaks in hot lard until
done, turning once.

SLAVE COOKING AND
THE HUMAN BOX

No one, especially anyone with Southern
roots, can deny the impact slaves had on Southern
cooking. Without the many culinary contributions
of slaves, Southern cooking would be bland and
nondescript. C.S.A. soldiers took their regional
cooking out onto the battlefields.
Slave cooks were highly resourceful. Meat
was secondary in slave cooking; vegetables and
grains were the main parts of most meals. Common
sense dictated this line of reasoning: vegetables
and grains were easy to come by, whereas the meat
supply was not always reliable.

Slave Quarters, Hampton Mansion
Towson, Maryland
(This slave quarters was by no means
indicative of most. This "luxury"
housing was considered grand and
palatial.)

The Underground Railroad, which operated from the 1830's to the 1860's, helped many slaves escape to Maryland, Pennsylvania, Ohio, New York and Canada (Canada was the ultimate destination of many slaves). Although Maryland held an equal number of free African-Americans and slaves, it was a border state, and many people were willing to help slaves. It was not unheard of for white people living in the actual Confederacy to help slaves escape, but consequences were dire if Southerners were caught helping slaves.

Desperate slaves went to great lengths and extreme personal peril to escape along the Underground Railroad. Some succeeded, others did not...

THE HUMAN BOX:

Henry Brown had had it with his so-called life... a living hell was more like it. Henry Brown wanted to escape slavery in the worst possible way, and he was quite willing to die in the process.

He escaped from the hated plantation and made his way to Richmond. Through the secret efforts of a white man, James A. Smith of that gentle city on the James River, Brown arranged to be packed in a 2'8"x3' wooden crate lined in felt. He was to be shipped to Philadelphia via the Adams Express Company in 1848 with the clothes on his back, water and some biscuits. The box was addressed to William A. Johnson.

When the time came, Brown sat in the box, and it was nailed shut. Brown must have been consumed with worry that he would be discovered enroute to freedom.

From Richmond, he was put on a train to Washington, D.C., then transferred to a train which would take him to Philadelphia. The entire trip would take 26 hours.

During Brown's journey, a telegram was delivered to Johnson which announced: "Your case of goods is shipped and will arrive tomorrow." The next morning, E.M. Davis, a member of the

Pennsylvania Anti-Slavery Society, recovered the crate from the Adams Express Office. An Adams driver brought the box to the anti-slavery office.

As Brown was released from the box, he sang a Psalm, "I waited patiently for the Lord, and he has heard my prayer."

Smith later crated two other slaves. His second attempt went awry when the human cargo was discovered. Smith consequently served eight years in prison. One hopes that Henry "Box" Brown lived happily ever after.

Hampton Mansion

SIDE DISHES

Slaves' contributions to cooking were most evident in the preparation of side dishes. Using imagination, resourcefulness, and foods at hand, slaves created some wonderful dishes.

Side dishes all too often became the main dish. As General Lee said, "The only unfailing friend the Confederacy ever had was cornfield peas". Union troops were not above using side dishes as an occasional meal, either. Sometimes rations were late, or sutlers ran low on desired items.

APPLESAUCE

5-10 apples, peeled
   and quartered
water
$\frac{1}{2}$-1 C sugar

Combine apples, water and sugar in a kettle; cook over medium heat 10-20 minutes (until tender). Mash left-over solids into a sauce with entire mix-ture. Serve warm or cold (some folks add milk to applesauce to make a sort of thick drink).

BAKED BEANS

1 pound dry navy beans
bacon or salt pork, cut up (optional, but
   great if available)
1 large onion, chopped
½ C molasses
¼ C sugar
salt and pepper

Pick over and rinse beans. Put beans in a Dutch
oven with water two to three inches over the beans.
Bring to boil, reduce heat, simmer for 2 minutes.
Remove from heat, cover and let stand one hour. Or,
don't boil the water and soak beans overnight in a
covered pot. Drain and rinse beans.

Add fresh water and boil; reduce heat. Cover and
simmer 1-1½ hours (until tender), stirring from
time to time. Drain beans; reserve liquid.

Add meat and onion; stir in one cup of reserved
bean liquid, molasses, sugar, salt and pepper.
Bake, uncovered at 300o for 2 hours, stirring
occasionally. Add more bean liquid if necessary.

BLACK-EYED PEAS

Pick over and rinse as many black-eyed peas as you
have; put them in a pot with enough water to cover.
Chop one or two onions and cut up some salt pork (if
salt pork is available) and throw it in the pot.

Boil peas for 15 minutes, then cover the pot
partially and simmer until the peas are tender --
about 1½ hours. Add water as needed, but do not
allow the peas to become watery. Add salt and
pepper before serving.

BUTTER BEANS

butter beans (about 2 pounds)
bacon (if available)
5 C water
sugar
salt and pepper

Pick over and rinse beans. Put beans in a pot with
2 or 3 inches of water to cover.

Cut up bacon, saute in butter for 10 minutes; drain
off fat. Add other ingredients and cook for 45
minutes (until done -- beans should be very soft),
adding water if needed.

CABBAGE (BOILED)

head of cabbage
salt and pepper

Remove wilted outer
leaves, wash cabbage.
Cut into four wedges or
into one-inch pieces.
Boil, uncovered, two
or three minutes.
Cover and cook 8-10
minutes for wedges
and 5-7 minutes for
pieces (texture should
be crisp yet tender --
boiled cabbage is ghastly
if overcooked).

CABBAGE (FRIED)

head of cabbage
lard
salt and pepper
$\frac{1}{4}$-$\frac{1}{2}$ C water

Remove wilted outer leaves, wash cabbage. Cut the
cabbage, lengthwise, into many strips (discard the
core). Put cabbage, lard and water into a cast iron
skillet, cover and cook slowly, stirring once in a
while, about 45-60 minutes. Don't let cabbage cook
dry, but add as little water as possible.

Increase heat to high, remove the lid and stir
constantly until the moisture is evaporated
and cabbage is a nice golden brown. Season with
salt and pepper before serving.

CATSUP

Catsup is not a side dish, but it was used during the War to add flavor to various foods. This version is not nearly as good as what is known in modern times. Neither side had ready access to cinnamon, cloves or red pepper, but cooks made do.

tomatoes, peeled and sliced
1 or 2 onions, finely chopped
vinegar (to taste)
sugar (to taste)
salt (to taste)

Combine tomatoes and onions, bring to boil; reduce heat, simmer, uncovered, 45 minutes, stir often. Remove from heat, strain mixture, reserve juice. Set aside.

If cinnamon or cloves are available, tie them in a cheesecloth bag and add to vinegar in a small pan. Bring to boil; reduce heat, simmer, uncovered, 30 minutes; discard spice bag. If spices are not available, skip this step (but you still need vinegar).

Cook reserved tomato juice, uncovered, over a medium-high heat two hours (until volume is reduced by half); stir often. Add vinegar, sugar and salt. Cook, uncovered, 30-40 minutes until thickened.

CORNBREAD AND MILK

This recipe sounds simple, but it was breakfast, lunch or supper more than once!

cornbread
buttermilk or milk

Crumble up cornbread into a cup or bowl of milk and enjoy.

CORNMEAL MUSH

Mush was sliced and fried, and eaten plain or preferably covered with molasses, butter or sugar.

6 C water
2 C cornmeal
salt
butter ($\frac{1}{4}$ of the size of an egg)
lard

Bring water to a boil; add salt, reduce heat to low, then **very** slowly add the cornmeal **steadily** while stirring constantly. Reduce heat to low (mixture should be bubbling); continue cooking, stirring all the while for 20-25 minutes until mixture is thick and smooth. Stir in butter.

Put the mixture into a flat pan and let cool. Then, cut mush into squares. Fry the squares in hot lard, turning once, until brown on both sides (3-5 minutes).

CREAMED POTATOES

2 pounds potatoes, peeled and cut into
    eighths
1 quart water
salt and pepper
butter ($\frac{1}{4}$ of an egg-size)
1 small onion, finely diced
$\frac{1}{4}$ C flour
3 C milk (**not** buttermilk)

Boil potatoes for 20-25 minutes (until done); drain. Heat butter in another pan, add onion and cook for 2-3 minutes. Stir in flour and cook 1 to 2 minutes; don't allow flour to brown. Add taters, stir in milk until smooth. Add salt and pepper.

FRIED APPLES

Apples
sugar
butter
water

Peel, core and slice apples; put them in a large
skillet. Add sugar and a bit of water. Fry apples
in butter until tender (25-30 minutes). Water must
be evaporated; do not let apples scorch.

FRIED CORN

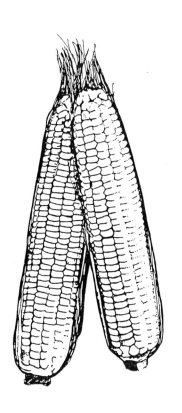

Ears of corn
salt and pepper
lard

In a bowl, scrape
kernels from ears of
corn, making **sure** to
reserve the milky
liquid. Fry the
corn mixture in hot
lard 10-12 minutes,
stirring often. At
the end of cooking,
season with salt and
pepper.

FRIED GREEN BEANS AND ONIONS

Green beans, cleaned and cut up
onions, chopped coarsely
butter (or lard, but butter is much better)

Saute onions in butter until transparent (7-10 minutes). Add green beans and quickly cook beans with onions until beans are about halfway done -- they should still be bright green and also **very** crispy. This is one time green beans should not be soggy and overcooked.

FRIED GREEN TOMATOES

Sliced green tomatoes (figure one tomato per man)
1 C cornmeal
salt and pepper
lard
1-3 C milk

Combine cornmeal, salt, pepper and milk. Dip each tomato slice in batter, letting excess batter drip in bowl. Fry in hot lard in skillet until browned, turning once.

FRIED POTATOES

Potatoes, peeled and sliced
onions (optional)
salt and pepper
lard

Fry potatoes and onions in lard until potatoes are browned. When potatoes are done, scrape out the brown pieces stuck to the bottom of the skillet and serve with the rest of the potatoes.

GRAVY

This is the kind of gravy that is served over biscuits, and no one ever said biscuits and gravy can't be served for supper!

Recipe:
2-4 tbs lard or bacon or sausage drippings*
2-4 tbs flour
salt and pepper
2-3 C milk (or water can be substituted for half the milk)

*Note: Modern-day cooks can use 2-4 tbs of vegetable oil. The gravy is just as good.

In a cast iron skillet, add flour to lard and stir into a roux. Cook the roux until it is the color of a copper penny. Some people don't like their gravy this dark, so stop cooking the roux once it reaches the desired color. Slowly add milk, stirring after each addition. Adding milk gradually and stirring well enables the gravy to reach the desired thickness. Cook gravy for 15-20 minutes, adding salt and pepper near the end of cooking.

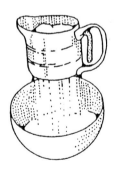

GREENS AND POT LIKKER

A mess of greens (turnip, collard, kale)
½ lb salt pork, cut up (optional)
salt
small handful of sugar
water (about 2 quarts)
2 or 3 tbs vinegar (optional)

Break stems off of greens below the leaf. Wash
greens in a large tub of water, repeat several
times in fresh water each time. Drain greens and
cut up coarsely.

Bring water, salt pork, salt and sugar to a boil in
a large pot. Add greens, cover and simmer 1-2 hours
to the desired tenderness. Serve with "pot likker"
(the cooking juice). Greens and pot likker are
especially good with crumbled up cornbread.

GRITS (HOMINY)

8 C grits
6 tbs butter
4 C water
2 C milk or water

Bring water to a boil, add butter. Stir in the
grits, return to a boil, and reduce heat. Cook
grits for 10 minutes, or until they are thick and
most of the water has been absorbed. Be sure to
stir grits from time to time to keep them from
sticking.

Add one cup of the milk or water, turn down heat
and simmer grits for about 10 minutes. As the
liquid disappears, add more, cooking grits until the
desired consistency is reached. The total cooking
time from start to finish should be about an hour.

HAM AND GREEN BEANS

Snap, pole or string beans
ham pieces or a ham hock
salt
water (about one pint)

Break tips off both ends of beans; wash and drain.
Combine salt, water and ham in a large pot. Cook
over medium heat until it boils. Lower heat, cover
the pot and let everything simmer for 15 minutes.

Bring to boil, add beans, boil again; reduce to a
simmer for 1-1½ hours. Beans should be very tender
-- almost "overdone." Cook until all water is gone,
stirring often to keep beans from scorching.

HOPPIN' JOHN

Hoppin' John can be eaten either as a side
dish or as a main dish, depending on whatever other
food is available. Meat does not have to be added
(if scarce) to this slave dish.

There are differing opinions as to the deri-
vation of the name "hoppin' john." Some folks say
that long-ago children, when hearing that the tasty
treat would be served that day, hopped around the
kitchen table in anticipation.

Other folks say husbands hopped around in
a light-hearted dance after supper because the food
was so good they couldn't help themselves. To
further complicate matters, some folks say the husband joyfully danced before the meal, and the children danced afterwards.

Others say that upon smelling the dish being
prepared, a neighborhood man hung around the kitchen
door, prompting the cook to call out, "Hop in, John!"

HOPPIN' JOHN

2 C black-eyed peas or cowpeas
10-12 C water
ham or bacon (optional)
2 onions, chopped
2 C rice
salt and pepper

Pick over and rinse the peas; put them in a pot.
Boil the peas, salt and pepper, meat and onion,
uncovered, 1½ hours (don't let peas get mushy).
Add rice to the pot, making sure there is about
4 C of water left in the pot. Cover and simmer
over low heat for 20 minutes.

Remove the pot from heat and let it sit for
about 15 minutes (keep pot covered).

MASHED TATERS

taters
butter
milk
salt and pepper

Wash and peel taters,
cut into chunks.
Boil 20-25 minutes or
until they can be
cleanly pierced with
a fork. Drain taters,
then mash with fork
until lumps are out.
Add butter, salt,
pepper and milk. If
milk is not available,
butter will have to
do.

OKRA

okra
flour or cornmeal
lard
salt and pepper

Wash okra and cut off tips and stem ends (do not
cut into the pod -- not even a little bit. Cutting
into the pod results in the milky discharge that
some folks find unappetizing). Cut the okra into
½-inch slices and put in a bowl. Dredge okra in
the flour or cornmeal and toss to coat well. Fry
okra in hot lard until brown. Season with salt and
pepper.

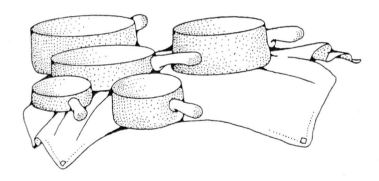

OKRA AND CORN FRY

4 or 5 ears of corn
1 large onion, chopped
1 C okra, tips and stems removed
    (remember, don't cut into the pods)
3 or 4 tomatoes, chopped
salt and pepper
butter or lard

Scrape kernels from the corn, reserving the
milky liquid to use in recipe. Heat butter or
lard. Stir in corn and onions and saute for
two or three minutes. Add remaining ingredients
and cover, cooking 3-5 minutes until okra is
tender. Uncover skillet and cook 2 minutes
longer (juice from tomatoes should nearly be
gone).

PEAS AND ONIONS

6 tbs butter
6 bunches green onions, chopped
9 C green peas
salt
3 C water

Melt butter, add onions. Cook onions but do
not let them brown. Add peas, salt and water.
Cover and simmer for 10 minutes, or until peas
are done.

POTATOES AND GREEN BEANS

green beans, stringed and broken in half
salt and pepper
potatoes
water to cover -- a couple of inches above
    beans

Put everything but the taters in a Dutch oven;
boil water and cook for ½ hour. Add taters, cook
for another ½ hour. Remove lid and cook until no
liquid remains (don't scorch).

POTATO PANCAKES

potatoes, peeled and finely diced
onions, diced
flour
salt and pepper
lard
1 egg

Combine everything (except lard). Heat lard in a
cast iron skillet. Shape tater mixture into small
cakes. Fry in lard just until golden brown.

POTATOES, TURNIPS AND ONIONS

10-12 turnips, peeled (parsnips can be
    substituted)
10-12 taters, peeled and cut up
10 onions, chopped
10-15 carrots, diced (optional)
lard, 12-15 tbs
water

Bring water to boil in kettle. Cook taters and
onions for 15 minutes with lard. Add everything
else and cook for 15-20 minutes until taters are
done.

101

RICE

2 C rice
4 C water
salt

Wash rice in a large
bowl until there is
no milkiness. Put
water, salt and rice
in a pot over medium
heat; bring to a boil.
Stir to keep rice
from sticking, but
do not stir rice
after this step is
complete. Reduce
heat to low; uncover
the pot just a wee bit.
Simmer rice for 12-15
minutes. Fluff the
rice, then completely
cover the pot and
cook for maybe
10 more minutes
(until all water
is gone).

ROASTED POTATOES

Cut white or sweet potatoes into quarters,
dredge in melted lard or butter, sprinkle with
salt and pepper. Put potatoes in a Dutch oven
and roast at 350o for one hour.

STEWED TOMATOES

tomatoes, peeled and quartered
½ C butter or lard
salt and pepper
cooked green beans (optional)

Heat lard or butter in a skillet; add tomatoes
and salt. Cover skillet and simmer tomatoes
over a low heat for about 20 minutes (until
tomatoes are tender). Stir from time to time,
and add pepper to taste at the end of cooking.
Green beans can be a delicious addition to the
stewed tomatoes. Some folks also like to add
boiled potatoes (add peeled and cut up potatoes
that have been boiled for about 10 minutes to
the stewing tomatoes).

SWEET POTATOES (FRIED)

sweet potatoes
lard
salt

Wash and peel the sweet potatoes. Cut potatoes
into thin round slices. Heat lard until very
hot. Fry the slices, a few at a time, until
slices are crisp and golden brown. Drain the
potatoes and season with salt.

SUCCOTASH

4 C dried lima beans
12 C boiling water
10-12 ears of corn
salt

Pick over and rinse lima beans. Put beans in
a large pot, and pour boiling water on them; let
sit for two hours. Meanwhile, scrape kernels
from the ears of corn over a bowl, reserving the
milky liquid.

Bring beans to a boil, then reduce heat to low
and cook for 1½-2 hours (until beans are tender).
Add water to keep beans covered with two or
three inches of water.

During the last 10 minutes of cooking, add corn
and milky liquid to the beans.

SUMMER SQUASH (FRIED)

summer squash
salt and pepper
breadcrumbs from biscuits **or** loose cornmeal

Wash, peel and slice squash crosswise. Dip in
crumbs or cornmeal. Fry in hot lard or butter
for 10-15 minutes, turning once in a while.

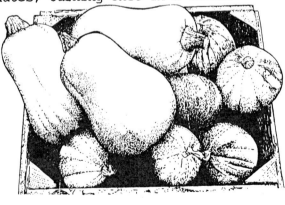

THE SEXY SPY

Most men are suckers for beautiful women, especially tragic young widows, and men of the Civil War era were no exceptions. A beautiful and intelligent Washington, D.C. socialite repeatedly wheedled sensitive and vital information to help the C.S.A.'s cause. Military leaders on both sides believed this living doll spy was largely responsible for the Union's totally unexpected butt-kicking at First Bull Run.

The woman was Rose O'Neal Greenhow, a lifelong resident of the Nation's Capitol. She had moved in society's elite circles all her adult life. Whether she was born into society, or whether she came from humble beginnings and reinvented herself or whether she married into society are not clear. No matter **how** she got there, she had in her lacy pocket top military officers, politicians, and U.S. Presidents.

The man thought to have persuaded her to become a spy was South Carolina's John C. Calhoun. Calhoun spent a lot of time with the young lovely after the death of her husband.

Washington's jaded society culture welcomed her antics like a breath of fresh air, and she was

A Southern Belle
Bull Run Battlefield

romantically dubbed "The "Wild Rose."

Lowly civil servants kow-towed to her, believing she could make or break the career of any man in Washington. Some fellows probably resented her but kept quiet. Her stooges fed her data

105

that could only hurt the U.S. Government and help the C.S.A.

She was a savvy person who understood battle plans and strategies. She communicated military plans quickly, managing to get these plans into the right hands.

Her cleverness at getting sensitive information where it needed to go was made more astonishing when faced with muddy battle plans used by generals such as Stonewall Jackson. Stonewall claimed his battlefield successes were because of "Mystery. Mystery is the secret of success." He sometimes sent troops forward without revealing their destination. Their leader would be told what route to take when the troops reached certain crossroads.

Stonewall's love of things mysterious came back to bite him after his death. One of the mysteries of the Civil War is why was Jackson's amputated left arm buried in its own grave, apart from the rest of his body? No one seems to know the answer! The best answer anyone can come up with is that his men, thinking he would survive after being shot accidentally by C.S.A. soldiers, planned to present him with his arm as a joke. Then, when he up and died on them, they had to do **something** with it. If he had been an enlisted man, it would have been tossed away, but his men could not bring themselves to be so disrespectful. Why the arm wasn't buried with the rest of Stonewall is unclear; it was buried by a minister in the graveyard of the minister's brother's plantation.

Rose warned the undermanned Beauregard of the coming Union threat at First Bull Run, and he was able to plan his defensive posts well enough to achieve victory. Afterward, Rose received an anonymous telegram saying the entire Confederacy was in her debt.

Cocky with victory and growing more full of herself, she too quickly expanded her spy network. Someone squealed on her (a spurned lover... a resentful civil servant... a jealous female neighbor???).

Rose was imprisoned for espionage and treason. She managed to send Beauregard, from prison, information that would help him in the Second Battle of Bull Run. How she managed to smuggle information out of prison is anyone's guess. When delivering information, she used her young daughter, a maid, or whomever else fell under her web of charm.

The United States did not want to hang her for treason. Their reluctance was not based on chivalry or on tender feelings towards the gentle sex. Rather, they feared scandal -- she might point the finger at high-falutin' male "friends". Many of Washington's movers and shakers were trembling in their boots, afraid Rose would spill the beans and destroy their careers.

It was decided that Rose would be shipped off to Richmond and warned not to do any more spying. That was like telling a cat not to play with a mouse. Rose laughed at the United States' stern instruction.

Jeff Davis, utterly dazzled by her, sent her off to Europe as a diplomatic courier. There, she continued to collect intelligence and send it back to Richmond. Then **one** day, she got some hot information she felt she could not trust to anyone else. She firmly believed she had to put it in Jeff Davis' hands herself.

She reached the Cape Fear River in North Carolina aboard a blockade runner, the Condor. There, she was not surprised (and was probably secretly thrilled, knowing Rose's love of thrills and adventure) to be chased by a Federal gunboat.

The Condor ran aground on a sandbar, and Greenhow had to get ashore to avoid having the Yankees find her military intelligence. She climbed into a lifeboat and made for the river-bank. The small craft floundered and was capsized by high waves.

This was clearly not Rose's day. She would surely have made it the few yards to shore **if** she had not been dragged down by her belt, which was heavy with two thousand dollars in gold.

Rather than remove the weighted belt, she allowed it to drag her under. The greedy beauty drowned, taking with her the gold and the urgent news for President Davis.

DESSERTS

Desserts were a haphazard affair on the battlefield. Cakes were seldom baked, and the men had to make do with a limited assortment of sweets.

BAKED APPLES

Peel and core apples; fill the cored holes with sugar, cinnamon and nutmeg (if spices are available). Bake at 375o for about 30 minutes, or until the apples are tender.

COBBLERS

Cobblers could use different types of fruit: blueberries, strawberries, peaches, apples, but the favorite fruit was blackberries. Two or three different kinds of fruits could be blended together and used in the same cobbler. No cobbler has ever suffered from having too much fruit.

There were three equally good ways of preparing fruit cobblers:

1) some folks liked to put a layer of pastry on the bottom of a pan (using half of the pastry dough) and the other half of the pastry over the fruit,
2) some cooks mixed the dough and the fruit together, or
3) other cooks put the fruit in the pan and then placed dollops of dough over the fruit.

Recipe for number one:
fruit - judge the quantity; 2 quarts black
    -berries, or 2 pints of blueberries,
    strawberries, peaches or apples sounds about
    right, but it really depended on how much
    fruit was available
3/4-1 C sugar
2 C flour
1 tsp salt
2/3 C plus 2 tbs lard
4 to 5 tbs very cold water

Sift together flour and salt. Cut lard into flour
until mixture looks like coarse meal. Sprinkle
water one tablespoon at a time over surface of
the mixture; stir with fork until dry ingredients
are moistened. Shape into a ball and keep as cold
as possible.

Roll or pat dough out to a ¼" thickness. Place
one-half of the dough on the bottom of a lightly
greased baking pan. Spread combined fruit and
sugar over pastry. Lay the other half of pastry
over fruit; brush **lightly** with butter. Make a few
steam slits in pastry, and bake at 375o for 20-25
minutes (until top is a light golden brown).

Recipe for number two:

fruit
1½ C flour
1 C sugar
1 C milk
butter (**not** lard) the size of an egg

Melt butter, pour into large bowl. Add remaining
ingredients, pour into lightly greased baking dish,
and bake at 350o for 20-25 minutes (until lightly
browned).

Recipe for number three:

Use the same recipe as for number two, but put
fruit and sugar (combined) into a lightly greased
baking pan and drop dollops of batter over fruit.
Bake at 350o for 20-25 minutes (until pastry is
lightly browned).

<u>COOKIES</u>

Battlefield cookies were a sorry state
of affairs. Ingredients were very basic, and few
sweet tooths were fully satiated. One doubts
many hands were reaching into the cookie jar.

1 C butter, melted
1-1½ C sugar
1 C milk (scant)
5 C flour
½ tsp baking soda
½ tsp cream of tartar

Mix butter and sugar, add milk. In another bowl,
combine flour, baking soda, and cream of tartar
and slowly add to the butter mixture; mix well.

Shape dough into 1½-inch balls and flatten each
ball with a floured fork. Bake 20-25 minutes in
a 375o oven. Don't let cookies get too brown.
Makes about 3 dozen.

CORN PUDDING

2 C corn kernels cut
   from cob (do not
   keep milky liquid)
3/4 C flour
3 tbs sugar
1 tsp salt
2 C milk
2 eggs, beaten
2 tbs butter (no
   lard!)

Combine corn, flour,
sugar, salt; stir well.
Combine remaining
ingredients, stir into
corn mixture.

Pour into a baking
pan that has been
lightly greased, and
bake at 350o for one
hour. Stir pudding
twice during the
first 30 minutes.

CUSTARDS (STIRRED AND BAKED)

6 C milk   4 eggs
1-1/3 C sugar   3 tbs flour

For stirred custard:
Cook milk until it is well heated; set aside.

Beat eggs until frothy; add sugar and flour,
beating until thick. Slowly stir in 1 C hot
milk into egg mixture; add to the remaining milk,
stirring constantly.

Cook custard over a low heat, stirring from time
to time, 30 minutes, or until thickened. Custard
can be served warm or cold.

For baked custard:
Skip step number three, and pour custard mixture
into a baking pan. Set baking pan in a larger
pan that has one inch of water in it.

Bake at 350o for 35-40 minutes, or until a knife
inserted in the center of the custard comes out
clean. Custard can be served warm or cold.

FRUIT PIES

Pies are another way in which various fruits could be used. Since most cooks had the basic ingredients on hand to make crusts (recipe follows at the end of the pie recipes), pies showed up often during months when fruits were in season.

APPLE PIE

Unbaked pastry for a double-crust pie
6 C peeled and sliced cooking apples
   (mixing two or three different kinds
    together makes the best apple pie)
3/4 C sugar
2 tbs flour
½ tsp cinnamon (if available)
4 tbs butter (**not** lard)

Roll half of pastry to a very thin thickness (1/8-inch) on a floured surface. Place in a 9-inch piepan.

Put apples in a large bowl. In another bowl, combine sugar, flour, spices and mix well. Spoon over apples, toss gently. Fill piepan with apple mixture and spread evenly; dot with butter.

Roll the other half of pastry to a 1/8-inch thickness; put on top of apples. Trim off excess pastry along edges. Fold edges under and flute. Cut a couple of steam vents in the top. Brush top of crust **lightly** with butter. Bake at 375o for one hour and ten minutes or until top is golden and fruit is tender.

BLACKBERRY PIE: Use 4 C berries, 1 C sugar, and 1/4 C flour (omit cinnamon). Bake for 45-50 minutes (until center of pie is firm).

BLUEBERRY PIE: Use 4 C berries, 3/4 C sugar, 3 tbs flour (omit cinnamon). Bake for 45-55 minutes (until center is firm).

CHERRY PIE: Use 4 C tart red pitted cherries, 1 C sugar, and 1/4 C flour (omit cinnamon). Cherry pie should be cooked at 400o for 60 minutes.

PEACH PIE: Use 6 C peeled, pitted and sliced peaches, 3/4 C sugar and 3 tbs flour (omit cinnamon).

PEAR PIE: Use 6 C peeled, cored and sliced pears, 1/2 C sugar and ¼ C flour (omit cinnamon). Bake for 40 minutes.

PLUM PIE

This plum pie is a one-pastry pie, as opposed to the other fruit pies which use two pastries. The recipe for a one-pastry pie follows.

8-10 plums
2 tbs flour
1 tsp cinnamon
2/3 C sugar
2 eggs, beaten

Cut plums into wedges, discarding pits. Put plums on pastry in bottom of a piepan. Sprinkle sugar and cinnamon over plums, then pour eggs over top evenly. Bake at 400o for 30 minutes.

The pastry recipe for plum pie is: 1¼ C flour, 2 tbs sugar, ½ C butter (melted), 1 tbs vinegar. Combine flour and sugar; add butter and vinegar, mix well. Roll pastry to fit a 10-inch piepan. Prick bottom with a fork and bake at 400o for 10 minutes.

RHUBARB PIE: Use 4 C rhubarb cut into one-inch pieces, 1 C sugar and ¼ C flour. Bake for 40 minutes or until crust is browned.

FRUIT PIE DOUBLE PASTRY

2 C flour
1 tsp salt
2/3 C lard (modern-day cooks can use solid
    shortening)
4 to 5 tbs cold water

Combine flour and salt; cut in lard until mixture resembles coarse meal. Sprinkle cold water over flour mixture a little at a time; stir with fork until dry mixture is moistened. Don't overwork dough, or it will get tough. Shape into a ball and keep as cold as possible.

INDIAN PUDDING

5 C scalded milk
1/3 C cornmeal
½ C molasses
2 tsp salt
2 tbs butter

Pour milk slowly on cornmeal and cook for twenty minutes. Add molasses, salt and melted butter; pour into a lightly greased baking pan and bake at 350 for 1-1½ hours. Pudding is done when a knife inserted in the center comes out clean.

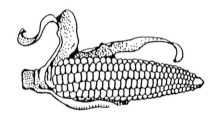

MOLASSES COOKIES

3/4 C lard
3/4 C sugar
1/4 C molasses
1 egg, beaten
2 C flour
2 tsp baking soda
1/2 tsp salt
1¼ tsp cinnamon

Melt lard; add sugar,
molasses and egg, blend
well. Add dry ingre-
dients and mix together
well. Make batter into
1" balls, put on lightly
greased baking surface.
Flatten cookies slightly
with a floured fork.
Bake at 350o for 10
minutes.

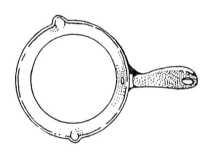

PUMPKIN PIE

2 C pumpkin (a small-medium whole pumpkin)
3/4 C sugar
½ C butter, softened
3 eggs
½ tsp cinnamon (if available)
¼ tsp salt
2/3 C evaporated milk (the North had evaporated
 milk; since the South did not, regular milk
 would be used)
½ C regular milk (add 2/3 C if evaporated milk
 is not available)
1 unbaked pastry shell (recipe follows)

Wash pumpkin and cut in half crosswise. Bake
halves, cut-side down on a gridiron at 325o
for 45 minutes (until fork comes out easily).
Cool slightly, peel pumpkin and discard seeds.
Mash well.

Combine pumpkin, sugar, butter, eggs, cinnamon,
and salt in large bowl. Beat until light; add
milk, beat until blended.

Pour mixture into a 10-inch pastry crust; bake
at 375o for 50-60 minutes or until a knife
inserted in the center comes out clean.

Single-shell pastry: 1-1/3 C flour, ½ tsp salt,
1/2 C lard, 3 to 4 tbs cold water.

Combine flour and salt; cut in butter until
mixture resembles coarse meal. Sprinkle cold
water, a little at a time, over surface. Stir
with fork until dry ingredients are moistened.
Shape into a ball; chill.

When ready to use, roll to a 1/8-inch thickness
and place in piepan, trimming off excess pastry
along edges; fold edges under and flute.

SPOONBREAD

4 C milk
1-1/3 C cornmeal
1½ tsp salt
1 tsp baking soda
1 tsp cream of tartar
2 tsp sugar
2 tbs butter, melted
6 eggs, separated

Scald milk; combine cornmeal, salt, baking soda, cream of tartar, and sugar. Slowly stir the dry mixture into the scalded milk and bring to a boil, stirring all the while.

Remove from heat; stir in butter. Beat egg yolks until thick and stir in one-fourth of the hot mixture, then stir yolk mixture into remaining cornmeal mixture. Beat egg whites until stiff peaks form, and fold into the cornmeal mixture.

Pour spoonbread into greased baking pan and bake at 350o for 25-30 minutes (until puffed and light brown). Since spoonbread is basically a cornmeal souffle, it must be served immediately.

SWEET POTATO PIE

2 C cooked and mashed sweet potatoes
1 C sugar
½ C butter, softened
2 eggs, separated
½ tsp cinnamon
¼ tsp salt
½ C evaporated milk (or regular)
¼ C sugar
1 unbaked 10-inch pie crust

Combine sweet potatoes, sugar, butter, egg yolks, cinnamon and salt in a large bowl; beat until light. Add milk and blend.

Beat egg whites until foamy, then slowly add sugar, a tablespoon at a time, beating until stiff peaks appear. Fold into the sweet potato mixture. Pour filling into the pastry shell and bake at 400o for 10 minutes; lower heat to 350o and bake another 45-50 minutes or until set.

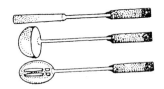

So, the long, bloody war seemed to finally be coming to an end. Soldiers on both sides were anxious to return home to their families -- to repair what had been broken and re-start their lives. Everyone had fought the good fight, but enough was enough.
Some of the fellows had children they had never seen, born after Pa marched bravely off to war.

It was April, 1865, and Grant had had Petersburg under siege for an incredible nine months, trying to choke off the railroads that were Lee's lifeline. Without the railroads, Lee was nothing, and he knew it. To further dishearten him, Sherman was marching through Georgia and South Carolina, creating complete devastation wherever he went.

Lee reluctantly abandoned Richmond and Petersburg, hoping to reach railways further south. Grant was not about to let Lee get away, and his troops headed him off.

THE NON-SURRENDER:

It is at this point that things grew fuzzy. Lee decided to seek an audience with Grant to see whether things could be worked out. Ever the Southern gentleman, he decked himself out in full dress uniform and met with Grant at Appomatox. Lee's insistence on looking sharp proved to be the Confederacy's downfall.

The two generals faced each other, and Lee was to look at some papers Grant had. Lee's sword bothered him as he sat, and he withdrew it. A hand quickly snaked out to grab the sword and Lee handed it over without looking at the owner of the

hand. Lee was startled as a loud collective whoop
went up from Yankees present. He looked at his
fellow Confederates, but they were as puzzled as he.

Grant told Lee he would gladly accept
Lee's gesture of surrender in handing over his
sword. Lee bristled and said, "Now, wait just a
darned minute. I'm not of a mind to surrender.
That sword was bothering me!"

Well, sir, at **that** point in time, Grant
and his men fell to the floor, they were laughing
so hard. They rolled around holding their sides
they were so merry! Grant managed to drag himself
to his feet in his dirty, mud-splattered uniform and
he fixed Lee with an evil eye. Grant intoned, "Are
we to understand that you are going back on your
surrender -- that you are not a man of your
word? Where is all this Southern gentleman
malarkey you are always spouting?... Or maybe
there is no such thing as a Southern **gentleman**."

Lee and his men cut their eyes at each
other, realizing it would be a bigger blow to the
pride of the entire C.S.A. if it appeared they
were going back on their word (which they weren't.
Lee never meant to surrender when he handed over
his sword. **That** thought was the farthest thing
from his mind).

When Lee appeared to be waffling, Grant
stepped forward with fists raised and snarled,
"Lee, maybe you're just a big sissy. Maybe we
ought to settle this **my** way."

Although the thought of knocking
Grant's block off held great appeal at that point
in time, Lee demurred. He motioned for his men
to join him in a corner of the room. Grant paced
back and forth like a caged tiger, wondering what
they were up to.

At last, Lee said he was surrendering.
Grant was jubilant. Lee **could** have stuck to his
guns and **insisted** that he was not surrendering, but
he and his loyal men agreed that even Grant should
not be allowed to look like a fool. In Southern
eyes, causing anyone to lose face is a sin and a

great disservice.

No, the C.S.A. would allow it to appear that they had surrendered. They were mighty tired of war anyway. They had no strength or heart to make a big deal out of Grant's erroneous assumption. The gracious men in gray would let sleeping dogs lie...

SUGGESTED READING

Davis, William. The Civil War Cookbook, Philadelphia, PA: Courage Books, 1993

Editors of Time-Life Books. Echoes of Glory: Arms and Equipment of the Confederacy, Alexandria, VA: Time-Life Books, 1991

Editors of Time-Life Books. Echoes of Glory: Arms and Equipment of the Union, Alexandria, VA: Time-Life Books, 1991

Fowler, Damon Lee. Classical Southern Cooking: A Celebration of the Cuisine of the Old South, New York, NY: Crown Publishers, 1995

Garrison, Webb. A Treasury of Civil War Tales, Nashville, TN: Rutledge Hill Press, 1988

Meade, Martha. Recipes From the Old South, New York, NY: Bramhall House, 1961

Shi, David E. and Tindall, George Brown. America, A Narrative History, New York, NY: W.W. Norton & Company, 1984

Taylor, John Martin. Hoppin' John's Lowcountry Cooking: Recipes and Ruminations from Charleston and the Carolina Coastal Plain, New York, NY: Bantam Books, 1992

Terdoslavich, William. The Civil War Trivia Quiz Book, New York, NY: The Fairfax Press, 1984

Darlene Funkhouser holds degrees in Law Enforcement and Business Management from the University of Maryland. She is a former newspaper reporter and once had a Hollywood screenplay agent. She lives in the Baltimore area, but spends as much time as possible in Florida and Virginia.

Need a Gift?

for

• Shower • Birthday • Mother's Day •
• Anniversary • Christmas•

Turn Page For Order Form
(Order Now While Supply Lasts!)

TO ORDER COPIES OF
Civil War Cookin', Stories 'n Such

Please send me _____copies of Civil War Cookin' at
$9.95 each plus $3.00 shipping and handling.
(Make checks payable to Quixote Press)

Name _____

Address _____

City _____State_____Zip_____

CALL 1-800-571-2665
QUIXOTE PRESS
3544 Blakslee Street
Wever, Iowa 52658

Please send me _____copies of Civil War Cookin' at
$9.95 each plus $3.00 shipping and handling.
(Make checks payable to Quixote Press)

Name _____

Address _____

City _____State_____Zip_____

CALL 1-800-571-2665
QUIXOTE PRESS
3544 Blakslee Street
Wever, Iowa 52658

NOTES

NOTES

NOTES

NOTES

NOTES

NOTES

NOTES

Contents

Foreword

Too often, swimmers without access to a good swim coach end up doing the same few workouts over and over again. Their workouts lack the structure needed to improve performance, not to mention the range and variety that make swimming fun. Even good coaches get stuck searching for new workout ideas. Nick and Eric Hansen have teamed up to give you *Workouts in a Binder® for Swimmers, Triathletes, and Coaches* to solve these problems.

Nick and Eric are top coaches by any measure, with years of experience coaching elite swimmers. By using this binder, you can measure and develop your performance with the same workouts utilized by national and Olympic swimmers. Nick and Eric have divided the workouts into categories and provided training plans so you can optimize your workout time to produce results— faster swimming. Of course, you can use the workouts to give you more variety even if performance is not your main goal.

Since publishing the first book in this series, we found that athletes interested in multiple stroke workouts wanted access to the same waterproof format that freestyle swimmers and triathletes have enjoyed for years. Additionally, supplementing freestyle workouts with multiple stroke workouts is an excellent strategy for an experienced triathlete's training plan. The creativity behind the Stroke and Individual Medley workouts in this binder meet those requests perfectly.

Workouts in a Binder® for Swimmers, Triathletes, and Coaches is an excellent complement to *Workouts in a Binder®: Swim Workouts for Triathletes.* Not only are the freestyle workouts in this booklet great for swimmers as well as for triathletes, they are all new.

I hope you enjoy the handy waterproof format. I know my athletes will all receive a copy so we can use the workouts as part of their training plans.

GALE BERNHARDT

2003 USA Triathlon Pan American
    Games Coach

2004 USA Triathlon Olympic Coach

Introduction

Welcome to *Workouts in a Binder*, workouts for swimmers, triathletes, and coaches. These unique workout cards are waterproof and can be used on the pool deck—no more moldy index cards in leaky plastic bags. The workouts are written so that yards or meters can be used in the instruction sets. Swimmers can use these cards to supplement their current workouts or use these to design their own workout plan. Several workout plans can be found on pages xiv–xviii.

This set of workouts can be used by competitive and noncompetitive swimmers. The workouts are divided into categories based on the characteristics of the main set. The categories are Distance (10), Middle Distance (15), Sprint (5), Individual Medley (10), and Stroke (10). Each workout features sets "A" and "B." The "A" main set is typically longer than the "B" main set.

All workouts include a warmup set, main set, and a cool-down. Choose either the "A" set or the "B" set depending on your ability and workout time. There are additional instructions for each workout at the end of the cool-down. These instructions should be read prior to starting the practice, and they should help eliminate any chance of boredom during the practice session.

It is our hope that the different types of workouts will help keep swimming interesting. Whether your goal is to compete or maintain fitness, we encourage you to try all of the workouts.

Types of Workouts

DISTANCE

The main emphasis of the distance workout is aerobic work. In general the main set contains longer swims with less rest. These longer swims are done at a moderate intensity. It is critical to maintain a pace that will allow you to complete the entire set.

MIDDLE DISTANCE

The main set is a combination of short swims mixed with longer swims. Often you will be changing speed and intensity throughout the set. It is critical that you do not always swim at a comfortable pace; you may be pushing yourself and feel uncomfortable.

SPRINT

These workouts are done at a very high intensity that will produce fast speeds. This type of work is considered anaerobic work and takes a lot of effort. It will also take some time once the set is completed to fully recover from the practice. Concentrate on good technique while you are giving a big effort.

INDIVIDUAL MEDLEY

The main set of the Individual Medley (IM) workouts demands a combination of all four strokes. Main sets will integrate IM swimming in conjunction with intervals of a specific stroke. By changing strokes these workouts will be a challenge. Everyone has a weak stroke, and these sets will allow you to turn your weakness into a strength.

STROKE

The main sets of the stroke workouts can be swum with any stroke except free. It is recommended not to change strokes during the practice but definitely to change strokes within a training plan.

Testing

It is important to complete a test set every three to four weeks to track your progress. These tests will result in establishing a pace for training to implement during your workouts. With training, your pace should get faster every three to four weeks. The following are two test sets:

Test A: Swim 3 × 300s with a 30-second rest between each one. Try and maintain the highest average speed possible. An accurate test is when all three 300s are within 15 seconds of each other. In other words, do not swim a fast first 300 followed by a third 300 that is slower by 20 seconds or more. Watch the clock and get your time on each 300. Average the time for all three 300s and divide the average by three to establish a pace per 100. For example, if you swam 3:30, 3:35, 3:22, the average time for 300 is 3:27. Divide that result by three to obtain a pace of 1:09.

Test B: Swim 3 × 100s with a 20-second rest between each one. The goal of the set is to swim at the highest possible sustained speed, achieving the lowest average time. In other words, do not swim a fast first 100 and then swim a third 100 that is 15 seconds slower. Try and keep the 100s all within 4 to 6 seconds. The test will not be accurate if the times are more than 10 seconds apart. Watch the clock and get your time on each 100. Average the 100s to establish a pace. For example, a reasonable swim might be 1:25, 1:21, and 1:24; the pace would be 1:23 per 100.

Use Chart 1 (on next page) to calculate your pace.

CHART 1: 300 Swim Pace

300 Average Time	PACE per 100	300 Average Time	PACE per 100
2:39	0:53	4:21	1:27
2:42	0:54	4:24	1:28
2:45	0:55	4:27	1:29
2:48	0:56	4:30	1:30
2:51	0:57	4:33	1:31
2:54	0:58	4:36	1:32
2:57	0:59	4:39	1:33
3:00	1:00	4:42	1:34
3:03	1:01	4:45	1:35
3:06	1:02	4:48	1:36
3:09	1:03	4:51	1:37
3:12	1:04	4:54	1:38
3:15	1:05	4:57	1:39
3:18	1:06	5:00	1:40
3:21	1:07	5:03	1:41
3:24	1:08	5:06	1:42
3:27	1:09	5:09	1:43
3:30	1:10	5:12	1:44
3:33	1:11	5:15	1:45
3:36	1:12	5:18	1:46
3:39	1:13	5:21	1:47
3:42	1:14	5:24	1:48
3:45	1:15	5:27	1:49
3:48	1:16	5:30	1:50
3:51	1:17	5:33	1:51
3:54	1:18	5:36	1:52
3:57	1:19	5:39	1:53
4:00	1:20	5:42	1:54
4:03	1:21	5:45	1:55
4:06	1:22	5:48	1:56
4:09	1:23	5:51	1:57
4:12	1:24	5:54	1:58
4:15	1:25	5:57	1:59
4:18	1:26	6:00	2:00

Definitions

BK: Backstroke

B-3, -4, -5: Breathe every third, fourth, or fifth stroke, respectively.

BEST AVG: Best average. The goal is to swim at the highest average speed possible, achieving the lowest average time.

BR: Breaststroke

BUILD: Get faster within the designated swim. For example, 25 build means to get faster throughout the entire 25 yards. The last 5 yards should be the fastest swimming of that particular 25.

C/D: Cool-down. Active swimming at a low intensity.

DESC: Descend the speeds of each swim. For example, on a set of 4 × 100s, each 100 is faster than the previous one.

DESC 2-2-2: Descend speed or go faster each two swims. For example, on a set of 6 × 100s, the first two are swum at a speed, the next two are faster, and the last two are the fastest.

DIST: Distance

DPS: Distance per stroke. Work on maximizing the distance each arm can propel the body. Count the number of strokes per 25.

DR: Your choice of drill. Examples include catch-up, fingertip drag, right arm, left arm, and sculling.

EASY: Swim with ease.

FAST: As fast as you can possibly swim for a given distance. Fast speed on a 50-yard swim will be faster than fast speed on a 200-yard swim.

FL: Butterfly

FR: Freestyle

F-TIP: Fingertip. Swim with your fingertips dragging on the surface of the water during the recovery phase of the stroke.

GOOD EFFORT: Swim with high intensity.

H-OUT: Swim with your head out of the water.

IM: Individual Medley—butterfly, backstroke, breaststroke, and freestyle, in that order.

K: Kick. No arms, kick only. Can be done with or without a kickboard. If kicking without a board, try to simulate normal swimming body position and keep arms streamlined.

LT: Left

MD: Middle distance

MOD: A moderate pace or moderate effort.

N/S: Negative split. The second half of the designated swim is faster than the first half of the swim.

PACE: The target speed that results from testing.

PACE −:01: Swim 1 second faster than pace. For example, if your pace was 1:10 per 100, then you would want to swim at 1:09 per 100.

PULL: Swim with a buoy. Paddles are optional.

RD: Round. One round is one time through a set that has to be repeated. Example: RD2 is second round or second time doing the set.

RI: Rest interval. Some swim sets will have a designated rest interval, such as (:25RI), which means a 25-second rest after each swim repetition.

RT: Right

SCULL: *Front:* In the prone position, your arms are stretched out in front of you. Hands scull in a figure eight to change pitches to propel you forward. Kick is minimal, with the head down or up.

Back: In the prone position, fingertips are pointing directly behind you. Do figure eights to propel your body forward.

SI: Some workouts will have a designated swim interval, which includes the swim time and the rest time. For example, 4 × 50s (1:00SI) represents leaving for a 50 on every 1:00.

SKP: Swim, kick, pull. For example, 200 SKP designates swimming a 200, kicking a 200, and then pulling a 200.

SP: Sprint. Swim at a higher effort and speed.

ST: Stroke. A stroke other than freestyle, either butterfly, backstroke, or breaststroke.

STDY: Steady. Swim at an even pace.

SW: Swim any stroke.

W/U: Warm-up segment, gently increasing speeds throughout. All workouts in this program have the same warm-up for both A-level and B-level swimmers.

WORKOUT PLAN: 13 Week Option A			
Week	Monday	Wednesday	Friday
1	DIST	IM	DIST
2	MD	DIST	ST
3	IM	MD	DIST
4	ST	DIST	MD
5	DIST	ST	SP
6	MD	IM	SP
7	DIST	SP	ST
8	MD	SP	SP
9	DIST	IM	MD
10	IM	SP	ST
11	SP	MD	SP
12	DIST*	SP*	SP*
13	SP*	SP*	RACE

*Reduce main set by half.

WORKOUT PLAN: 13 Week Option B			
Week	Monday	Wednesday	Friday
1	DIST	IM	DIST
2	DIST	IM	MD
3	DIST	ST	DIST
4	MD	ST	DIST
5	MD	IM	DIST
6	MD	SP	MD
7	IM	ST	SP
8	SP	DIST	SP
9	MD	SP	IM
10	MD	ST	SP
11	SP	MD	SP
12	SP*	ST*	SP*
13	MD*	SP*	RACE

*Reduce main set by half.

WORKOUT PLAN: 13 Week Option C			
Week	Monday	Wednesday	Friday
1	DIST	IM	DIST
2	DIST	IM	DIST
3	MD	DIST	IM
4	MD	DIST	IM
5	DIST	ST	MD
6	DIST	ST	MD
7	IM	SP	MD
8	SP	IM	SP
9	MD	DIST	SP
10	SP	MD	SP
11	DIST*	IM	SP*
12	SP*	MD*	IM*
13	SP*	SP*	RACE

*Reduce main set by half.

WORKOUT PLAN: 26 Week Option A

Week	Monday	Wednesday	Friday
1	DIST	IM	DIST
2	DIST	ST	DIST
3	DIST	DIST	IM
4	DIST	DIST	ST
5	DIST	MD	DIST
6	IM	DIST	MD
7	DIST	MD	DIST
8	ST	DIST	MD
9	DIST	IM	MD
10	DIST	MD	ST
11	DIST	IM	MD
12	DIST	MD	ST
13	MD	DIST	IM
14	MD	ST	DIST
15	MD	DIST	IM
16	MD	ST	DIST
17	DIST	IM	MD
18	MD	ST	SP
19	SP	IM	MD
20	MD	SP	DIST
21	SP	MD	SP
22	SP	IM	SP
23	MD*	DIST*	ST*
24	SP	IM*	SP
25	SP*	MD*	SP*
26	SP*	SP*	RACE

*Reduce main set by half.

WORKOUT PLAN: 26 Week Option B

Week	Monday	Wednesday	Friday
1	DIST	DIST	DIST
2	DIST	IM	DIST
3	DIST	DIST	DIST
4	DIST	MD	DIST
5	IM	DIST	ST
6	DIST	MD	DIST
7	DIST	IM	ST
8	DIST	MD	DIST
9	MD	IM	DIST
10	DIST	MD	ST
11	MD	IM	DIST
12	DIST	MD	ST
13	MD	SP	IM
14	MD	SP	ST
15	MD	SP	IM
16	MD	SP	ST
17	SP	IM	MD
18	DIST	SP	SP
19	SP	IM	MD
20	MD	SP	SP
21	ST	SP	MD
22	SP	IM	SP
23	SP	MD*	SP
24	DIST*	SP	IM*
25	SP	MD*	SP*
26	SP*	SP*	RACE

*Reduce main set by half.

WORKOUT PLAN: 26 Week Option C			
Week	Monday	Wednesday	Friday
1	DIST	IM	DIST
2	DIST	IM	DIST
3	DIST	MD	DIST
4	DIST	IM	MD
5	DIST	MD	DIST
6	DIST	IM	DIST
7	MD	DIST	IM
8	DIST	MD	DIST
9	MD	IM	MD
10	DIST	MD	SP
11	MD	IM	SP
12	DIST	MD	SP
13	MD	SP	MD
14	DIST	SP	SP
15	MD	SP	MD
16	DIST	SP	SP
17	DIST	MD	SP
18	IM	MD	SP
19	SP	MD	SP
20	IM	MD	SP
21	MD	MD	DIST*
22	SP	IM	SP
23	MD	SP	IM*
24	MD	SP	SP
25	SP*	MD*	SP*
26	SP*	SP*	RACE
*Reduce main set by half.			

Distance Free 1A

W/U: **12 × 75** [3 × (FR, K NO BOARD, BK/BR/FR, B-4)]

WORKOUT A

2X			– 2:00 bonus rest –
3 × 250 DESC 1–3	(:20RI)		
2 × 250 100	(:10RI)	**800**	PULL N/S
50	(:10RI)		
50	(:10RI)		
50	(:40RI)		

C/D: **100** FR, **100** BK   TOTAL: **4400**

INSTRUCTIONS: **Work hard on the broken 250s.**

WORKOUT **B**

Distance Free 1B

W/U: **12** × **75** [3 × (FR, K NO BOARD, BK/BR/FR, B-4)]

3 × 250 DESC 1–3	(:20RI)	— 2:00 bonus rest —
1 × 250 100	(:10RI)	
50	(:10RI)	
50	(:10RI)	
50	(:40RI)	
2X		**400** PULL N/S

C/D: **100** FR, **100** BK   TOTAL: **3500**
INSTRUCTIONS: **Work hard on the broken 250s.**

Distance Free 2A

W/U: 3 × 400 (200 FR, 100 IM, 100 K)

4 × 100 DESC 1-4	(:20RI)	**4 × 100** K		(:15RI)
– 1:00 bonus rest –		**4 × 100** BEST AVG		(:20RI)
1 × 400 GOOD EFFORT		– 2:00 bonus rest –		
– 1:00 bonus rest –		**12 × 75** SW		(:15RI)
8 × 50 DESC 2-2-2-2	(:15RI)		75 BUILD	
– 1:00 bonus rest –		4X	75 EASY	
1 × 400 GOOD EFFORT			75 MOD ST	
– 1:00 bonus rest –				

C/D: 100   TOTAL: **4600**

INSTRUCTIONS: **Make sure the 100s within the 400s are all the same.**

WORKOUT A

3

WORKOUT **B**

Distance Free 2B

W/U: **3 × 400** (200 FR, 100 IM, 100 K)

4 × 100	DESC 1–4	(:20RI)	
	– 1:00 bonus rest –		
1 × 200	GOOD EFFORT		
	– 1:00 bonus rest –		
8 × 50	DESC 2-2-2-2	(:15RI)	
	– 1:00 bonus rest –		
1 × 200	GOOD EFFORT		
	– 1:00 bonus rest –		

4 × 100	K	(:15RI)
2 × 100	BEST AVG	(:20RI)
	– 2:00 bonus rest –	
6 × 75	SW	(:15RI)

2X
$\left[\begin{array}{l} \text{75 BUILD} \\ \text{75 EASY} \\ \text{75 MOD ST} \end{array}\right.$

C/D: **100**   TOTAL: **3550**

INSTRUCTIONS: **Make sure the 100s within the 200s are all the same.**

Distance Free 3A

W/U: **300** SW, **100** SCULL, **200** SW, **100** SCULL, **100** SW, **100** SCULL

WORKOUT A

5 × 200	DESC to 85%	(:20RI)	**200**	FAST	(1:00RI)
200	FAST	(1:00RI)	**2 × 200**	DESC to 85%	(:20RI)
4 × 200	DESC to 85%	(:20RI)	**200**	FAST	(1:00RI)
200	FAST	(1:00RI)	**200**	EASY	(1:00RI)
3 × 200	DESC to 85%	(:20RI)	**200**	FAST	

C/D: **400** EASY   TOTAL: **5300**

INSTRUCTIONS: **100% effort on the fast 200s.**

WORKOUT **B**

Distance Free 3B

W/U: **300** SW, **100** SCULL, **200** SW, **100** SCULL, **100** SW, **100** SCULL

4 × 200 DESC to 85%	(:20RI)	**200** FAST	(1:00RI)
200 FAST	(1:00RI)	**1 × 200** DESC to 85%	(:20RI)
3 × 200 DESC to 85%	(:20RI)	**200** EASY	(1:00RI)
200 FAST	(1:00RI)	**200** FAST	(1:00RI)
2 × 200 DESC to 85%	(:20RI)		

C/D: **400** EASY   TOTAL: **4300**

INSTRUCTIONS: **100% effort on the fast 200s.**

6

Distance Free 4A

W/U: **300** FR, **200** K, **200** PULL, **200** SW

4 × 150	(:10RI)	**1 × 400** N/S	
2 × 300 N/S	(:30RI)	— 2:00 bonus rest —	
2 × 200	(:15RI)	**4 × 250** PULL	(:20RI)

C/D: **300** TOTAL: **4200**

INSTRUCTIONS: **Negative split the longer swims by 10 seconds.**

Distance Free

WORKOUT **B**

Distance Free 4B

W/U: **300** FR, **200** K, **200** PULL, **200** SW

3 × 150	(:10RI)	**1 × 400** N/S
2 × 300 N/S	(:15RI)	– 2:00 bonus rest –
1 × 200	(:15RI)	**4 × 200** PULL (:20RI)

C/D: **300**   TOTAL: **3650**

INSTRUCTIONS: **Negative split the longer swims by 10 seconds.**

Distance Free 5A

W/U: **300** FR, **100** SCULL, **200** FR, **100** SCULL, **100** FR, **100** SCULL
2 × 300 (50 K, 100 DR, 150 SW EACH 50 FASTER) (:15RI)

4 × 200 N/S DESC	(:15RI)	**2 × 200** N/S DESC	(:15RI)
200 FAST	(:25RI)	**400** FAST	(:25RI)
3 × 200 N/S DESC	(:15RI)	**1 × 200** N/S	(:15RI)
300 FAST	(:25RI)	**500** FAST	

C/D: **300**   TOTAL: **5200**
INSTRUCTIONS: **N/S DESC**—second 100 1–3 seconds faster.

WORKOUT A

Distance Free

WORKOUT B

Distance Free 5B

W/U: **300** FR, **100** SCULL, **200** FR, **100** SCULL, **100** FR, **100** SCULL
2 × 300 (50 K, 100 DR, 150 SW EACH 50 FASTER) (:15RI)

4 × 150	N/S DESC	(:20RI)	2 × 150	N/S DESC	(:20RI)
200	FAST	(:30RI)	200	FAST	(:30RI)
3 × 150	N/S DESC	(:20RI)	1 × 150	N/S	(:20RI)
200	FAST	(:30RI)	200	FAST	(:30RI)

C/D: **300**   TOTAL: **4100**
INSTRUCTIONS: **N/S DESC**—second 75 1–2 seconds faster.

Distance Free 6A

W/U: **300** SW, **100** SCULL, **200** SW, **100** SCULL, **200** SW, **100** SCULL, **100** SW, **100** SCULL

2X			200	EASY
3 × 100 50 K, 50 SW	(:15RI)		**20 × 50** ODDS EASY,	EVENS FAST (:20RI)
2 × 150 N/S DESC	(:15RI)			
300 PULL DESC 100s	(:20RI)			
600 200 STDY, 100 FAST	(:20RI)			

C/D: **200**   TOTAL: **5300**

INSTRUCTIONS: **50 K, 50 SW** — a kickboard is optional but highly recommended.

Distance Free 6B

WORKOUT B

W/U: **300** SW, **100** SCULL, **200** SW, **100** SCULL, **100** SW, **100** SCULL

	2X	200	EASY
3 × 100	50 K, 50 SW	(:15RI)	
2 × 100	N/S DESC	(:15RI)	**12 × 50** ODDS EASY, EVENS FAST (:20RI)
200	PULL DESC 50s	(:20RI)	
400	150 STDY, 50 FAST	(:20RI)	

C/D: **200**   TOTAL: **4100**

INSTRUCTIONS: **50 K, 50 SW**—a kickboard is optional but highly recommended.

12

Distance Free 7A

W/U: **400** SW, **200** K, **400** SW, **200** PULL,
12 × 50 BUILD EVERY 3RD 50 (:10RI)

30 × 100   (:30RI)

    1–12   EVERY 3RD BEST AVG
   13–22 EVERY OTHER BEST AVG
   23–30 ALL BEST AVG

200   EASY

4 × 250   PULL DESC 1–4   (:20RI)

C/D: **300**   TOTAL: **6300**
INSTRUCTIONS: **Prepare yourself mentally and have a best average time goal.**

WORKOUT A

WORKOUT B

Distance Free 7B

W/U: **400** SW, **200** K, **400** SW, **200** PULL,
12 × 50 BUILD EVERY 3RD 50 (:10RI)

20 × 100   (:30RI)
  1–9   EVERY 3RD BEST AVG
  10–17   EVERY OTHER BEST AVG
  18–20   ALL BEST AVG

200   EASY

4 × 150 PULL DESC 1–4   (:20RI)

C/D: **300**   TOTAL: **4900**
INSTRUCTIONS: **Prepare yourself mentally and have a best average time goal.**

Distance Free 8A

W/U: **600** SW, **600** (50 K, 50 SW, 200 DR, 50 K, 50 DR, 200 SW),
3 × 250 [25 K, 25 SW (:10RI), 25 DR, 25 SW (:10RI), 150 N/S (:20RI)]

3 × 400	DESC	(:20RI)
3 × 300	DESC	(:20RI)
3 × 200	DESC	(:20RI)
3 × 100	DESC	(:20RI)

C/D: **250**   TOTAL: **5200**

INSTRUCTIONS: **Descend to 90% on the 400s, 300s, 200s, and 100s.**

WORKOUT **A**

Distance Free

Distance Free 8B

WORKOUT B

W/U: **600** SW, **600** (50 K, 50 SW, 200 DR, 50 K, 50 DR, 200 SW),
3 × 250 [25 K, 25 SW (:10RI), 25 DR, 25 SW (:10RI), 150 N/S (:20RI)]

3 × 200	DESC	(:20RI)
4 × 150	DESC	(:20RI)
5 × 100	DESC	(:20RI)
6 × 50	DESC	(:20RI)

C/D: **250**   TOTAL: **4200**
INSTRUCTIONS: **Descend to 90% on the 400s, 300s, 200s, and 100s.**

16

Distance Free 9A

W/U: **400** SW, **200** K, **200** PULL, **400** SW

600	N/S	(:30RI)	**2 × 100**	DESC	(:30RI)
2 × 300	DESC	(:20RI)	**100**	N/S	(:30RI)
400	N/S	(:30RI)	**2 × 50**	DESC	(:20RI)
2 × 200	DESC	(:20RI)	**100**	EASY	(:30RI)
200	N/S	(:30RI)	**5 × 100**	BEST AVG	(:30RI)

C/D: **200**   TOTAL: **4600**

INSTRUCTIONS: **Descend to 95% and set a goal for the best average 100s.**

WORKOUT A

17

WORKOUT B

Distance Free 9B

W/U: **400** SW, **200** K, **200** PULL, **400** SW

400	N/S	(:30RI)	**2 × 100**	DESC	(:30RI)
2 × 200	DESC	(:20RI)	**100**	N/S	(:30RI)
300	N/S	(:30RI)	**2 × 50**	DESC	(:20RI)
2 × 150	DESC	(:20RI)	**100**	EASY	(:30RI)
200	N/S	(:30RI)	**4 × 100**	BEST AVG	(:30RI)

C/D: **200**   TOTAL: **3900**

INSTRUCTIONS: **Descend to 95% and set a goal for the best average 100s.**

Distance Free 10A

W/U: **300** SW, **100** SCULL, **200** SW, **100** SCULL, **100** SW, **100** SCULL (:15RI)

600	N/S	(:20RI)	**1 × 200**	FAST	
3 × 200	DESC	(:20RI)	**100**	EASY	
400	N/S	(:20RI)	**3 × 500**	PULL, B-3, BUILD	(:20RI)
2 × 200	DESC	(:20RI)			
200	N/S	(:40RI)			

C/D: 200 TOTAL: **5100**

INSTRUCTIONS: **Swim the 500s with an aggressive effort.**

Distance Free

Distance Free 10B

WORKOUT B

W/U: **300** SW, **100** SCULL, **200** SW, **100** SCULL, **100** SW,
100 SCULL (:15RI)

500	N/S		(:20RI)	100	N/S		(:40RI)
3 × 100	DESC		(:20RI)	1 × 100	FAST		
300	N/S		(:20RI)	3 × 300	PULL, B-3, BUILD		
2 × 100	DESC		(:20RI)				(:20RI)

C/D: **200**   TOTAL: **3500**

INSTRUCTIONS: **Swim the 300s with an aggressive effort.**

Middle Distance Free 1A

W/U: **200** SW, **3 × 300** (100 K NO BOARD, 100 SW, B-3, 100 REVERSE IM)

4 × 75	BUILD and DESC	(:20RI)	1 × 100 EASY	(1:00RI)
1 × 200	at PACE	(:30RI)	4 × 100 at PACE	(:20RI)
4 × 100	BUILD and DESC	(:20RI)	– 2:00 bonus rest –	
1 × 300	at PACE	(:30RI)	16 × 25 ODDS BUILD ST,	
4 × 150	PULL	(:20RI)	EVENS 20-YARD SP	
1 × 400	at PACE	(:30RI)	(:30 or :40SI)	

C/D: **200**   TOTAL: **4400**

INSTRUCTIONS: **Choose and hold a pace that will allow you to make the entire set.**

WORKOUT A

Middle Distance Free

21

Middle Distance Free 1B

WORKOUT B

W/U: **200** SW, **3 × 300** (100 K NO BOARD, 100 SW, B-3, 100 REVERSE IM)

4 × 75	BUILD and DESC	(:20RI)	1 × 100	EASY		(1:00RI)
1 × 200	at PACE	(:30RI)	3 × 100	at PACE		(:20RI)
3 × 100	BUILD and DESC	(:20RI)		– 2:00 bonus rest –		
1 × 300	at PACE	(:30RI)	8 × 25	ODDS BUILD ST,		
3 × 150	PULL	(:20RI)		EVENS 20-YARD SP		
				(:35 or :45SI)		
1 × 400	at PACE	(:30RI)				

C/D: **200**   TOTAL: **3850**

INSTRUCTIONS: **Choose and hold a pace that will allow you to make the entire set.**

Middle Distance Free 2A

W/U: **300** SW, **4 × 50** (25 F-TIP, 25 K) (:15RI), **4 × 75** (50 BUILD, 25 K) (:15RI), **4 × 100** (50 EASY, 50 BUILD) (:20RI)

5 × 100 at PACE	(:20RI)	**1 × 400**	1ST 200 at PACE, 2ND 200 PACE –:02	
1 × 200 at PACE	(:20RI)		– 1:00 bonus rest –	
5 × 200 PACE –:02	(:30RI)	**200**	PULL	(:20RI)
1 × 200 at PACE	(:20RI)	**5 × 50**	SW w/PADDLES	(:20RI)
5 × 100 at PACE	(:30RI)			

C/D: **200**   TOTAL: **4650**

INSTRUCTIONS: **Focus on pace and make sure you are 2 seconds faster than pace on the five 200s and also on the second 200 of the 400.**

23

Middle Distance Free 2B

WORKOUT B

W/U: **300** SW, **4 × 50** (25 F-TIP, 25 K) (:15RI), **4 × 75** (50 BUILD, 25 K)
(:15RI), **4 × 100** (50 EASY, 50 BUILD) (:20RI)

3 × 100 at PACE	(:20RI)	1 × 400 1ST 200 at PACE, 2ND 200 PACE –:02
1 × 200 at PACE	(:30RI)	
3 × 200 PACE –:02	(:20RI)	– 1:00 bonus rest –
1 × 200 at PACE	(:30RI)	200 PULL (:20RI)
3 × 100 at PACE	(:20RI)	5 × 50 SW w/PADDLES (:20RI)

C/D: **200**   TOTAL: **3850**
INSTRUCTIONS: **Focus on pace and make sure you are 2 seconds faster than pace on the three 200s and also on the second 200 of the 400.**

Middle Distance Free 3A

W/U: **300** SW, **300** K, **300** IM DR

4X

2 × 150 85%	(:15RI)
1 × 150 PULL	(:15RI)

– 1:00 bonus rest –

3X

2 × 150 PULL 85%	(:15RI)
1 × 150 SW	(:30RI)

C/D: **200** SCULL, **200** FR   TOTAL: **4450**

INSTRUCTIONS: **Pull with a buoy; paddles are optional.**

Middle Distance Free

25

Middle Distance Free 3B

WORKOUT B

W/U: **300** SW, **300** K, **300** IM DR

3X			2X		
2 × 150	85%	(:15RI)	2 × 150	PULL 85%	(:15RI)
1 × 150	PULL	(:15RI)	1 × 150	SW	(:30RI)

— 1:00 bonus rest —

C/D: **200** SCULL, **200** FR   TOTAL: **3550**

INSTRUCTIONS: **Pull with a buoy; paddles are optional.**

Middle Distance Free 4A

W/U: **600** SW, **300** K

16 × 75 SW	(:15RI)		**3X**	
		100	SW	(:20RI)
4X [1–FR 1–ST 1–[25 BK, 25 BR, 25 FR] 1–K NO BOARD		**200**	SW	(:30RI)
		300	SW	(1:00RI)

– 2:00 bonus rest –

C/D: **300** (50 FR, 50 BK)   TOTAL: **4200**

INSTRUCTIONS: **Keep an even pace on the longer swims, but do not slow down when the distance increases.**

Middle Distance Free

Middle Distance Free 4B

W/U: **600** SW, **300** K

16 × 75 SW   (:15RI)

4X
[
1–FR
1–ST
1–[25 BK, 25 BR, 25 FR]
1–K NO BOARD
]

— 2:00 bonus rest —

		2X
100	SW	(:30RI)
200	SW	(:40RI)
300	SW	(1:00RI)

C/D: **300** (50 FR, 50 BK)   TOTAL: **3600**

INSTRUCTIONS: **Keep an even pace on the longer swims, but do not slow down when the distance increases.**

Middle Distance Free 5A

W/U: **3 × 150** (100 SW, 50 K) (:20RI), **3 × 150** (100 SW, 50 DR) (:20RI), **3 × 150** (100 ST, 50 BUILD FR) (:20RI)

4 × 75 BUILD to 90%	(:20RI)	**1 × 200** FAST	(1:00RI)
1 × 200 FAST	(1:00RI)	**1 × 100** EASY	
4 × 100 K BUILD to 90%	(:20RI)	– 2:00 bonus rest –	
1 × 200 FAST	(1:00RI)	**1 × 600**	
4 × 150 PULL BUILD to 90% (:20RI)		4X [100 FR MOD / 50 BUILD ST	

C/D: **200** EASY   TOTAL: **4150**

INSTRUCTIONS: **Each individual rep to 90% on BUILD sets.**

Middle Distance Free

29

WORKOUT B

Middle Distance Free 5B

W/U: **3 × 150** (100 SW, 50 K) (:20RI), **3 × 150** (100 SW, 50 DR) (:20RI), **3 × 150** (100 ST, 50 BUILD FR) (:20RI)

4 × 75	BUILD to 90%	(:20RI)	**1 × 100** FAST	(1:00RI)
1 × 100 FAST	(1:00RI)	**1 × 100** EASY	
4 × 100 K BUILD to 90%	(:20RI)	– 2:00 bonus rest –	
1 × 100 FAST	(1:00RI)	**1 × 600**	
2 × 150 PULL BUILD to 90% (:20RI)		2X [100 FR MOD / 50 BUILD ST	

C/D: **200** EASY   TOTAL: **3550**

INSTRUCTIONS: **Each individual rep to 90% on BUILD sets.**

Middle Distance Free 6A

W/U: **200** SW, **4 × 50** (25 H-OUT, 25 DPS) (:15RI), **4 × 50** (25 F-TIP, 25 DPS) (:15RI), **4 × 50** B-3 (:15RI), **4 × 50** B-4 (:15RI), **4 × 50** B-5 (:15RI)

3 × 100	MOD	(:20RI)	– 1:00 bonus rest –
3 × 100	at PACE	(:20RI)	**20 × 25** (ON:35)
2 × 200	MOD	(:30RI)	4X ⌈ 1 – BUILD
2 × 200	at PACE	(:30RI)	1 – SP
1 × 300	MOD	(:45RI)	1 – SP
1 × 300	at PACE		1 – B-4
			⌊ 1 – EASY

C/D: **200**   TOTAL: **3900**

INSTRUCTIONS: **Really attack the 25s at the end of the main set.**

WORKOUT **A**

31

Middle Distance Free 6B

WORKOUT B

W/U: **200** SW, **4 × 50** (25 H-OUT, 25 DPS) (:15RI), **4 × 50** B-3 (:15RI), **4 × 50** (25 F-TIP, 25 DPS) (:15RI), **4 × 50** B-4 (:15RI), **4 × 50** B-5 (:15RI)

3 × 100	MOD	(:20RI)	
3 × 100	at PACE	(:20RI)	— 1:00 bonus rest —
1 × 200	MOD	(:30RI)	**20 × 25** (ON:40)
2 × 150	at PACE	(:30RI)	⎡ 1 – BUILD
1 × 200	MOD	(:45RI)	4X ⎢ 1 – SP
			⎢ 1 – SP
1 × 200	at PACE		⎢ 1 – B-4
			⎣ 1 – EASY

C/D: **200**   TOTAL: **3400**

INSTRUCTIONS: **Really attack the 25s at the end of the main set.**

Middle Distance Free 7A

W/U: 200 SW, **2 × 300** (100 IM DR, 4 × 50 PULL B-4) (:10RI)

4 × 200 DESC 1–4	(:30RI)	**4 × 100** at PACE	(:15RI)
100 EASY		**100** EASY	
3 × 200 DESC 1–4	(:30RI)	**12 × 50**	(1:00SI)
100 EASY		4X [1–BUILD 1–FAST 1–EASY]	
2 × 200 PACE –:03	(:30RI)		
100 EASY			

C/D: 100 FR, **100** BK   TOTAL: **4200**

INSTRUCTIONS: **PACE –:03**—Swim each 100 3 seconds under pace.

WORKOUT **A**

Middle Distance Free

Middle Distance Free 7B

WORKOUT **B**

W/U: **200** SW, **2 × 300** (100 IM DR, 4 × 50 PULL B-4) (:10RI)

3 × 200	DESC 1–4	(:30RI)	**4 × 100**	at PACE	(:15RI)
100	EASY		**100**	EASY	
2 × 200	DESC 1–4	(:30RI)	**12 × 50**		(1:00SI)
100	EASY			1 – BUILD	
1 × 200	PACE –:03	(:30RI)	4X	1 – FAST	
100	EASY			1 – EASY	

C/D: **100** FR, **100** BK   TOTAL: **3600**

INSTRUCTIONS: **PACE** –:03—Swim each 100 3 seconds under pace.

34

Middle Distance Free 8A

W/U: **200** FR, **4 × 150** (50 K, 50 BUILD, 50 ST) (:10RI)

3 × 600	200 FR, 100 K, 200 N/S, 100 K	(:45RI)
4 × 150	50 EASY, 50 FAST, 50 MOD	(:20RI)
5 × 100	at PACE	(:20RI)
	– 2:00 bonus rest –	
8 × 50	K (ODD FAST, EVEN EASY)	(:15RI)

C/D: **300** (25 FR, 25 K ON BACK, 25 ST)   TOTAL: **4400**

INSTRUCTIONS: **Make quick transitions between kicking and swimming in the 600s (no rest).**

Middle Distance Free

Middle Distance Free 8B

WORKOUT B

W/U: **200** FR, **4 × 150** (50 K, 50 BUILD, 50 ST) (:10RI)

2 × 600	200 FR, 100 K, 200 N/S, 100 K	(:45RI)
4 × 150	50 EASY, 50 FAST, 50 MOD	(:20RI)
5 × 100	at PACE	(:20RI)
	– 2:00 bonus rest –	
8 × 50	K (ODD FAST, EVEN EASY)	(:15RI)

C/D: **300** (25 FR, 25 K ON BACK, 25 ST)   TOTAL: **3800**

INSTRUCTIONS: **Make quick transitions between kicking and swimming in the 600s (no rest).**

Middle Distance Free 9A

W/U: **600** (4 × 100 FR, 50 ST)

100	PACE –:02	(:20RI)	4 × 50	PACE –:01	(:10RI)
200	MOD	(:20RI)	300	PULL	(:30RI)
2 × 100	PACE –:02	(:20RI)	6 × 50	PACE –:01	(:10RI)
300	MOD	(:30RI)	400	EASY	
3 × 100	PACE –:02	(:20RI)		– 2:00 bonus rest –	
400	MOD	(:40RI)		⎡ 25 SPRINT, 25 EASY	
2 × 50	PACE –:01	(:10RI)	2X	2 × 25 SPRINT (:35SI), 25 EASY	
200	K	(:20RI)		⎣ 3 × 25 SPRINT, 25 EASY	

C/D: **200**   TOTAL: **4250**

INSTRUCTIONS: **Know your paces before starting the main set and adjust your speed accordingly.**

37

Middle Distance Free 9B

Middle Distance Free

W/U: **600** (4 × 100 FR, 50 ST)

100	PACE –:02	(:20RI)
100	MOD	(:20RI)
2 × 100	PACE –:02	(:20RI)
200	MOD	(:30RI)
3 × 100	PACE –:02	(:20RI)
300	MOD	(:40RI)
2 × 50	PACE –:01	(:10RI)
200	K	(:20RI)
4 × 50	PACE –:01	(:10RI)
200	PULL	(:30RI)
6 × 50	PACE –:01	(:10RI)
200	EASY	
	– 2:00 bonus rest –	
2 × ⎡ 2 × 25 SPRINT, 25 EASY ⎤		
⎢ 2 × 25 SPRINT (:45SI), 25 EASY ⎥		
⎣ 3 × 25 SPRINT, 25 EASY ⎦		

C/D: **200**   TOTAL: **3650**

INSTRUCTIONS: **Know your paces before starting the main set and adjust your speed accordingly.**

38

Middle Distance Free 10A

W/U: **300** SW, **200** (50 K, 50 DR, 50 K, 50 DR), **200** (50 DR, 50 SW, 50 DR, 50 SW)

150 50 K, 50 DR, 50 DPS	(:20RI)	**2X**	
250 50 K, 50 DR, 100 DPS	(:20RI)	**3 × 100** DESC	(:15RI)
250 50 K, 50 DR, 150 BUILD		**300** at PACE	(:15RI)
		150 50 SW, 50 K, 50 SW	(:15RI)
		150 50 K, 50 SW, 50 K	(:30 RI)
		16 × 25 ODD DR, EVEN FAST	(:25 RI)

C/D: **200**   TOTAL: **3750**

INSTRUCTIONS: **Descend the 100s to pace and hold that pace during the 300.**

Middle Distance Free

39

WORKOUT **B**

Middle Distance Free 10B

W/U: **300** SW, **200** (50 K, 50 DR, 50 K, 50 DR),
200 (50 DR, 50 SW, 50 DR, 50 SW)

150	50 K, 50 DR, 50 DPS	(:20RI)
200	50 K, 50 DR, 100 DPS	(:20RI)
250	50 K, 50 DR, 150 BUILD	

		2X	
3 × 100	DESC		(:15RI)
300	at PACE		(:15RI)
150	50 SW, 50 K, 50 SW		(:15RI)
150	50 K, 50 SW, 50 K		(:30 RI)
8 × 25	ODD DR		(:25 RI)
	EVEN FAST		

C/D: **200**   TOTAL: **3500**

INSTRUCTIONS: **Descend the 100s to pace and hold that pace during the 300.**

Middle Distance Free 11A

W/U: **300** FR, **3 × 100** (50 K, 50 SW) (:10RI), **300** FR, **3 × 100** (50 DR, 50 SW) (:10RI)

4 × 100 70–75%	(:15RI)	**2 × 150** 70–75–80% by 50	(:15RI)
2 × 150 70–75–80% by 50 (:15RI)		**4 × 100** 85–90%	(:20RI)
4 × 100 75–80%	(:15RI)	**200** EASY	(1:00 RI)
2 × 150 70–75–80% by 50 (:15RI)		**400** FAST N/S	
4 × 100 80–85%	(:20RI)		

C/D: **200 EASY**   TOTAL: **4500**

INSTRUCTIONS: **70% = 70% effort, 80% = 80% effort.**

Middle Distance Free

41

WORKOUT B

Middle Distance Free 11B

W/U: **300** FR, **3 × 100** (50 K, 50 SW) (:10RI), **300** FR,
3 × 100 (50 DR, 50 SW) (:10RI)

3 × 100 70–75%	(:15RI)	**1 × 150** 70–75–80% by 50	(:15RI)
1 × 150 70–75–80% by 50	(:15RI)	**3 × 100** 85–90%	(:20RI)
3 × 100 75–80%	(:15RI)	**200** EASY	(1:00 RI)
1 × 150 70–75–80% by 50	(:15RI)	**300** FAST N/S	
3 × 100 80–85%	(:20RI)		

C/D: **200** EASY   TOTAL: **3550**

INSTRUCTIONS: **70% = 70% effort, 80% = 80% effort.**

42

Middle Distance Free 12A

W/U: **200** SW, **200** K, **200** SW, **2 × 100** K (:10RI), **200** SW, **4 × 50** K (:10RI)

2 × 75 25 K, 25 DR, 25 SW (:15RI)	**600** EACH 200 FASTER (:15RI)
200 EACH 50 FASTER (:15RI)	**2 × 75** 25 K, 25 DR, 25 SW (:15RI)
2 × 75 25 K, 25 DR, 25 SW (:15RI)	**400** EACH 100 FASTER (1:00RI)
400 EACH 100 FASTER (:15RI)	**2 × 75** 25 K, 25 DR, 25 SW (:15RI)
2 × 75 25 K, 25 DR, 25 SW (:15RI)	**200** EACH 50 FASTER

C/D: **300** TOTAL: **4050**

INSTRUCTIONS: **Be sure to change speeds on the straight swims.**

WORKOUT A

Middle Distance Free 12B

WORKOUT B

W/U: **200** SW, **200** K, **200** SW, **2 × 100** K (:10RI), **200** SW,
4 × 50 K (:10RI)

2 × 75	25 K, 25 DR, 25 SW	(:15RI)	**400**	EACH 100 FASTER	(:15RI)
100	EACH 25 FASTER	(:15RI)	**2 × 75**	25 K, 25 DR, 25 SW	(:15RI)
2 × 75	25 K, 25 DR, 25 SW	(:15RI)	**200**	EACH 50 FASTER	(1:00RI)
200	EACH 50 FASTER	(:15RI)	**2 × 75**	25 K, 25 DR, 25 SW	(:15RI)
2 × 75	25 K, 25 DR, 25 SW	(:15RI)	**100**	EACH 25 FASTER	

C/D: **300**   TOTAL: **3250**
INSTRUCTIONS: **Be sure to change speeds on the straight swims.**

Middle Distance Free 13A

W/U: **300** FR, **4 × 150** (50 K, 50 DR, 50 SW) (:15RI), **200** K,
6 × 75 K (25 RT, 25 LT, 25 BK) (:15RI), **3 × 150** DESC by 50s (:15RI)

6X

100	MOD	(:20RI)
100	N/S	(:30RI)
100	MOD	(:20RI)
100	FAST	(:30RI)

C/D: **200**   TOTAL: **4600**

INSTRUCTIONS: **Push yourself on the fast 100s.**

WORKOUT **B**

Middle Distance Free 13B

W/U: **300** FR, **4 × 150** (50 K, 50 DR, 50 SW) (:15RI), **200** K,
6 × 75 K (25 RT, 25 LT, 25 BK) (:15RI), **3 × 150** DESC by 50s (:15RI)

	4X	
100	MOD	(:20RI)
100	N/S	(:30RI)
100	MOD	(:20RI)
100	FAST	(:30RI)

C/D: **200**   TOTAL: **3800**
INSTRUCTIONS: **Push yourself on the fast 100s.**

Middle Distance Free 14A

W/U: **300** SW, **200** (25 K, 25 SW), **300** SW, **200** (25 DR, 25 SW), **6 × 100** K DESC EVEN 100s (:20RI)

	3X	
3 × 50		(:10RI)
3 × 100	DESC	(:15RI)
3 × 50		(:10RI)
300	N/S	(:20RI)

C/D: **200**   TOTAL: **4500**

INSTRUCTIONS: **Descend 100s to pace and swim faster than pace on the 300.**

Middle Distance Free 14B

WORKOUT **B**

W/U: **300** SW, **200** (25 K, 25 SW), **300** SW, **200** (25 DR, 25 SW),
6 × 100 K DESC EVEN 100s (:20RI)

	3X
3 × 50	(:15RI)
2 × 100 DESC	(:20RI)
3 × 50	(:15RI)
300 N/S	(:20RI)

C/D: **200**   TOTAL: **4200**

INSTRUCTIONS: **Descend 100s to pace and swim faster than pace on the 300.**

Middle Distance Free 15A

W/U: **200** SW, **200** K, **200** PULL, **100** SW, **100** K, **100** PULL

400	PULL	(:25RI)	**1 × 75**	25 K, 25 DR, 25 SW	(:20RI)
300	PULL	(:15RI)	**1 × 75**	FAST	(:30RI)
400	PULL	(:25RI)	**2 × 50**	25 K, 25 DR	(:20RI)
2 × 200	PULL, DESC	(:15RI)	**2 × 50**	FAST	(:30RI)
400	PULL	(:25RI)	**4 × 25**	K	(:20RI)
3 × 100	PULL, DESC	(:15RI)	**4 × 25**	FAST	(:30RI)

– 2:00 bonus rest –

C/D: **250** TOTAL: **3900**

INSTRUCTIONS: **Try pulling with paddles and buoy; do not use your legs while pulling.**

WORKOUT B

Middle Distance Free 15B

W/U: **200** SW, **200** K, **200** PULL, **100** SW, **100** K, **100** PULL

300	PULL	(:25RI)	**1 × 75**	25 K, 25 DR, 25 SW	(:20RI)
200	PULL	(:15RI)	**1 × 75**	FAST	(:30RI)
300	PULL	(:25RI)	**2 × 50**	25 K, 25 DR	(:20RI)
2 × 150	DESC	(:15RI)	**2 × 50**	FAST	(:30RI)
300	PULL	(:25RI)	**4 × 25**	K	(:20RI)
4 × 50	PULL, DESC	(:15RI)	**4 × 25**	FAST	(:30RI)

– 2:00 bonus rest –

C/D: **250**   TOTAL: **3300**

INSTRUCTIONS: **Try pulling with paddles and buoy; do not use your legs while pulling.**

Sprint Free 1A

W/U: **400** SW, **3 × 150** (25 K RT, 25 RT ARM, 25 K LT, 25 LT ARM, 50 DPS) (:15RI)

3X		2X
4 × 50 DESC :02 to 95% (:15RI)		**4 × 50** K DESC 1–4 (:15RI)
2 × 100 PACE –:04 and PACE –:06 (:15RI)		**1 × 300** PULL (:30RI)
– 0:30 bonus rest –		– 1:00 bonus rest –
1 × 200 DESC 50s to 100%		

C/D: **200** TOTAL: **3850**

INSTRUCTIONS: **Set target speeds prior to starting the main set.**

WORKOUT **A**

Sprint Free

Sprint Free 1B

W/U: **400** SW, **3 × 150** (25 K RT, 25 RT ARM, 25 K LT, 25 LT ARM, 50 DPS) (:15RI)

	3X	
4 × 50	DESC :02 to 95% (:15RI)	
2 × 100	PACE −:04 and	
	PACE −:06 (:15RI)	
	— 0:30 bonus rest —	
1 × 200	DESC 50s to 100%	

— 1:00 bonus rest —

4 × 50   K DESC 1–4   (:15RI)

1 × 300 PULL (:30RI)

C/D: **200**   TOTAL: **3350**

INSTRUCTIONS: **Set target speeds prior to starting the main set.**

Sprint Free 2A

W/U: 300 FR, **6 × 75** PULL (:15RI), **200** ST, **6 × 50** PULL ST (:15RI)

4X

1 × 75	RT ARM, LT ARM, BUILD	(:15RI)
1 × 50	FAST	(:20RI)
2 × 50	K MOD	(:15RI)
1 × 75	RT ARM, LT ARM, BUILD	(:15RI)
2 × 50	FAST	(:20RI)
4 × 50	K MOD	(:15RI)

– 1:00 bonus rest –

16 × 25 (:30 or :40SI)

4X
- 1 – EASY
- 1 – EASY/FAST
- 1 – EASY
- 1 – FAST

C/D: 200 (50 FR, 50 BK)   TOTAL: **4250**

INSTRUCTIONS: **Change strokes on each round of the 25s at the end of the main set.**

Sprint Free

Sprint Free 2B

WORKOUT B

W/U: **300** FR, **6 × 75** PULL (:15RI), **200** ST, **6 × 50** PULL ST (:15RI)

	3x	
1 × 75	RT ARM, LT ARM, BUILD	(:15RI)
1 × 50	FAST	(:20RI)
2 × 50	K MOD	(:15RI)
1 × 75	RT ARM, LT ARM, BUILD	(:15RI)
2 × 50	FAST	(:20RI)
4 × 50	K MOD	(:15RI)

— 1:00 bonus rest —

	16 × 25	(:30 or :40SI)
4X	1 – EASY	
	1 – EASY/FAST	
	1 – EASY	
	1 – FAST	

C/D: **200** (50 FR, 50 BK)   TOTAL: **3650**

INSTRUCTIONS: **Change strokes on each round of the 25s at the end of the main set.**

Sprint Free 3A

W/U: **300** SW, **300** K, **300** (25 IM, 25 FR, 25 IM), **200** SW, **200** K, **200** IM (25 DR, 25 K)

			2X			
1 × 200	N/S	(:30RI)	**3 × 50**	FAST	(1:00SI)
1 × 100	N/S	(:20RI)	**1 × 100**	EASY	
1 × 50	FAST	(1:00SI)	**5 × 50**	FAST	(1:00SI)
1 × 100	N/S	(:20RI)			

C/D: **300**   TOTAL: **3700**

INSTRUCTIONS: **Set a goal on the fast 50s and maintain that speed.**

WORKOUT A

Sprint Free

Sprint Free 3B

W/U: **300** SW, **300** K, **300** (25 IM, 25 FR, 25 IM), **200** SW, **200** K,
200 IM (25 DR, 25 K)

			2X		
1 × 200	N/S	(:30RI)	**3 × 50**	FAST	(1:30SI)
1 × 100	N/S	(:20RI)	**1 × 100**	EASY	
1 × 50	FAST	(1:30SI)	**5 × 50**	FAST	(1:30SI)
1 × 100	N/S	(:20RI)			

C/D: **300**   TOTAL: **3700**

INSTRUCTIONS: **Set a goal on the fast 50s and maintain that speed.**

Sprint Free 4A

W/U: **400** SW, **6 × 75** (25 K RT, 25 K LT, 25 DPS) (:20RI)

100	SW EACH 25 FASTER (:20RI)	**1 × 100** N/S		(:15RI)
75	25 DR, 25 SW, 25 DR (:25RI)	**3 × 200** EACH 50 FASTER		(:25RI)
25	FAST (:30RI)		3X	
3 × 100 N/S	(:15RI)			
200	EACH 50 FASTER (:25RI)	**50**	DR	(:20RI)
2 × 100 N/S	(:15RI)	**50**	FAST	(:40RI)
2 × 200 EACH 50 FASTER (:25RI)		**25**	DR	(:20RI)
		25	FAST	(:30RI)

C/D: **250**   TOTAL: **3550**

INSTRUCTIONS: **Be aware of the changing speeds throughout the set.**

Sprint Free

57

Sprint Free 4B

WORKOUT B

W/U: **400** SW, **6 × 75** (25 K RT, 25 K LT, 25 DPS) (:20RI)

100	SW EACH 25 FASTER (:20RI)	**1 × 100**	N/S	(:15RI)
75	25 DR, 25 SW, 25 DR (:25RI)	**3 × 200**	EACH 50 FASTER	(:25RI)
25	FAST		— 1:00 bonus rest —	
	(:30RI)			
3 × 100	N/S (:15RI)	**50**	DR	(:20RI)
200	EACH 50 FASTER (:25RI)	**50**	FAST	(:40RI)
2 × 100	N/S (:15RI)	**25**	DR	(:20RI)
2 × 200	EACH 50 FASTER (:25RI)	**25**	FAST	(:30RI)

C/D: **250**   TOTAL: **3250**

INSTRUCTIONS: **Be aware of the changing speeds throughout the set.**

Sprint Free

Sprint Free 5A

W/U: **400** SW, **6 × 75** (25 K RT, 25 K LT, 25 DPS) (:20RI)

100	SW EACH 25 FASTER (:20RI)	**3 × 200** EACH 50 FASTER	(:25RI)
75	25 DR, 25 SW, 25 DR (:25RI)	– 1:00 bonus rest –	
25	FAST (:30RI)	**3X**	
3 × 100 N/S (:15RI)		**50** DR	(:20RI)
200	EACH 50 FASTER (:25RI)	**50** FAST	(:40RI)
2 × 100 N/S (:15RI)		**25** DR	(:20RI)
2 × 200 EACH 50 FASTER (:25RI)		**25** FAST	(:30RI)
1 × 100 N/S (:15RI)			

C/D: **250** TOTAL: **3550**

INSTRUCTIONS: **Use the first half of the main set to tune up for the sprints.**

Sprint Free

59

Sprint Free 5B

WORKOUT B

W/U: **400** SW, **6 × 75** (25 K RT, 25 K LT, 25 DPS) (:20RI)

100	SW EACH 25 FASTER (:20RI)		1 × 100	N/S (:15RI)
75	25 DR, 25 SW, 25 DR (:25RI)		3 × 200	EACH 50 FASTER (:25RI)
25	FAST (:30RI)			– 1:00 bonus rest –
3 × 100	N/S (:15RI)	50	DR	(:20RI)
200	EACH 50 FASTER (:25RI)	50	FAST	(:40RI)
2 × 100	N/S (:15RI)	25	DR	(:20RI)
2 × 200	EACH 50 FASTER (:25RI)	25	FAST	(:30RI)

C/D: **250**   TOTAL: **3250**

INSTRUCTIONS: **Use the first half of the main set to tune up for the sprints.**

Individual Medley 1A

W/U: **150** FR, **150** K, **150** FR, **150** PULL, **8 × 50** (25 IM, 25 FR) (:15RI)

150 FL/FR/BK/FR/BR/FR (:20RI)	**4 × 100** 2 at 90%, 2 at 95%
4 × 75 80%, 85%, 90%, 95% (:20RI)	**200** EASY
2 × 150 FL/FR/BK/FR/BR/FR (:20RI)	– 2:00 bonus rest –
8 × 75 2 each (80%, 85%, 90%, 95%) (:20RI)	2X
4 × 100 IM (:20RI)	**1 × 300** PULL (:20RI)
	4 × 25 SPRINT (:45RI)

C/D: 100 TOTAL: **4250**

INSTRUCTIONS: **Choice of stroke on the 75s. The set of eight 75s can each be a different stroke.**

Individual Medley

61

Individual Medley 1B

W/U: **150** FR, **150** K, **150** FR, **150** PULL, **8 × 50** (25 IM, 25 FR) (:15RI)

150	FL/FR/BK/FR/BR/FR (:20RI)	**4 × 100** 2 at 90%, 2 at 95%	
4 × 75	80%, 85%, 90%, 95% (:20RI)	**200** EASY	
2 × 150	FL/FR/BK/FR/BR/FR (:20RI)	— 2:00 bonus rest —	
8 × 75	2 each (80%, 85%, 90%, 95%) (:20RI)	**1 × 300** PULL (:20RI)	
4 × 100	IM (:20RI)	**4 × 25** SPRINT (:45RI)	

C/D: **100**   TOTAL: **3850**

INSTRUCTIONS: **Choice of stroke on the 75s. The set of eight 75s can each be a different stroke.**

Individual Medley

Individual Medley 2A

W/U: **200** SW, **3 × 200** [1 × 50 DPS, 2 × 25 K, 4 × 25 IM (:15RI)]

2 × 50	FR BUILD	(:15RI)		**2 × 50**	FR BUILD	(:15RI)
1 × 100	IM	(:20RI)		**1 × 300**	IM	(:20RI)
1 × 200	FR PULL	(:30RI)		**1 × 200**	FR PULL	
2 × 50	FR BUILD	(:15RI)			– 2:00 bonus rest –	
1 × 200	IM	(:20RI)		**3 × 400**	25 FR, 25 IM	(:30RI)
1 × 200	FR PULL	(:30RI)				

C/D: **200**   TOTAL: **3700**

INSTRUCTIONS: **Even pace on the 400s (FR/IM).**

WORKOUT A

Individual Medley

63

Individual Medley 2B

WORKOUT **B**

W/U: **200** SW, **3 × 200** [1 × 50 DPS, 2 × 25 K, 4 × 25 IM (:15RI)]

2 × 50	FR BUILD	(:15RI)	2 × 50	FR BUILD	(:15RI)
1 × 100	IM	(:30RI)	1 × 300	IM	(:30RI)
1 × 200	FR PULL	(:30RI)	1 × 200	FR PULL	
2 × 50	FR BUILD	(:15RI)			
1 × 200	IM	(:30RI)	— 2:00 bonus rest —		
1 × 200	FR PULL	(:30RI)	2 × 400	25 FR, 25 IM	(:30RI)

C/D: **200**   TOTAL: **3300**
INSTRUCTIONS: **Even pace on the 400s (FR/IM).**

Individual Medley 3A

W/U: **600** SW, **6 × 75** (25 DR, 25 K, 25 SW) (:15RI)

1 × 50 25 FL, 25 BK	(:10RI)	**4 × 75** 25 BK, 25 BR, 25 FR (:15RI)
2 × 75 25 FL, 25 BK, 25 BR (:15RI)		**6 × 100** 50 BK, 25 BR, 25 FR (:20RI)
3 × 100 50 BK, 25 BR, 25 FR (:20RI)		**1 × 400** N/S
1 × 200 FR N/S	(:40RI)	– 1:00 bonus rest –
2 × 50 25 FL, 25 BK	(:10RI)	**800** PULL DESC 200s

C/D: **100**   TOTAL: **4050**

INSTRUCTIONS: **This is a great practice for stroke transitions.**

Individual Medley

65

Individual Medley 3B

WORKOUT B

W/U: **600** SW, **6 × 75** (25 DR, 25 K, 25 SW) (:15RI)

1 × 50	25 FL, 25 BK	(:10RI)	**4 × 75** 25 BK, 25 BR, 25 FR (:15RI)
2 × 75	25 FL, 25 BK, 25 BR	(:15RI)	**4 × 100** 50 BK, 25 BR, 25 FR (:20RI)
2 × 100	50 BK, 25 BR, 25 FR	(:20RI)	**1 × 400** N/S
1 × 200	FR N/S	(:40RI)	– 1:00 bonus rest –
2 × 50	25 FL, 25 BK	(:10RI)	**400** PULL DESC 200s

C/D: **100**   TOTAL: **3350**

INSTRUCTIONS: **This is a great practice for stroke transitions.**

66

Individual Medley 4A

W/U: **200** SW, **100** IM K, **100** IM DR, **200** SW, **100** IM K, **100** IM DR, **200** IM

2 × 150 50 FL, 50 BK, 50 BR (:15RI)		**2 × 100** 50 FL, 50 BK	(:15RI)
100 FR	(:20RI)	**200** FR	(:20RI)
2 × 150 50 BK, 50 BR, 50 FR (:15RI)		**2 × 100** 50 BR, 50 FR	(:15RI)
100 FR	(:30RI)	**200** FR	(:30RI)
2 × 200 IM FAST	(:40RI)	**400** IM FAST	

C/D: **300**   TOTAL: **3700**

INSTRUCTIONS: **It's good practice to work on turns and transitions.**

Individual Medley

67

WORKOUT **B**

Individual Medley 4B

W/U: **200** SW, **100** IM K, **100** IM DR, **200** SW, **100** IM K,
100 IM DR, **200** IM

2 × 100	50 FL, 50 BK	(:15RI)	2 × 75	25 FL, 25 BK, 25 BR (:15RI)
100	FR	(:20RI)	150	FR (:20RI)
2 × 100	50 BR, 50 FR	(:15RI)	2 × 75	25 BK, 25 BR, 25 FR (:15RI)
100	FR	(:30RI)	150	FR (:30RI)
3 × 100	IM FAST	(:40RI)	2 × 200	IM FAST (:40RI)

C/D: **300**   TOTAL: **3200**

INSTRUCTIONS: **It's good practice to work on turns and transitions.**

Individual Medley 5A

W/U: **300** SW, **200** IM (25 K, 25 DR), **100** SCULL,
3 × 50 (FL/BK, BK/BR, BR/FR) (:10RI)

200	IM		**300**	IM	(:20RI)
300	FR	(:20RI)	**400**	FR	(:15RI)
300	IM	(:15RI)	**400**	IM	(:20RI)
200	FR	(:20RI)	**300**	FR	
	FR	(:15RI)			

C/D: **250**   TOTAL: **3400**

INSTRUCTIONS: **Keep a steady pace and use good stroke technique.**

Individual Medley

Individual Medley 5B

W/U: **300** SW, **200** IM (25 K, 25 DR), **100** SCULL,
3 × 50 (FL/BK, BK/BR, BR/FR) (:10RI)

100	IM	(:20RI)	200	IM	(:20RI)
200	FR	(:15RI)	300	FR	(:15RI)
200	IM	(:20RI)	3 × 100	IM	(:20RI)
100	FR	(:15RI)	200	FR	

C/D: **250**   TOTAL: **2600**
INSTRUCTIONS: **Keep a steady pace and use good stroke technique.**

Individual Medley 6A

W/U: **500** SW, **300** IM (25 K, 25 DR, 25 SW), **3 × 100** IM (:10RI)
3 × 50 K, **50** PULL, **2 × 50** K, **2 × 50** PULL, **50** K, **3 × 50** PULL (:10RI)

WORKOUT A

		3X		
75	25 FL, 25 BK, 25 BR (:15RI)		**75**	25 FR, 25 FL, 25 BK (:15RI)
75	25 BK, 25 BR, 25 FR (:15RI)		**200**	FR (:20RI)
75	25 BR, 25 FR, 25 FL (:15RI)		**200**	IM (:20RI)

C/D: **200**   TOTAL: **4000**

INSTRUCTIONS: **Increase your speed each round with a 90–95% effort on the third round.**

Individual Medley

Individual Medley 6B

W/U: **500** SW, **300** IM (25 K, 25 DR, 25 SW), **3 × 100** IM (:10RI)
3 × 50 K, **50** PULL, **2 × 50** K, **2 × 50** PULL, **50** K, **3 × 50** PULL (:10RI)

		3X		
50	25 FL, 25 BK	(:15RI)	**50**	25 FR, 25 FL	(:15RI)
50	25 BK, 25 BR	(:15RI)	**200**	FR	(:20RI)
50	25 BR, 25 FR	(:15RI)	**2 × 100**	IM	(:20RI)

C/D: **200**   TOTAL: **3700**
INSTRUCTIONS: **Increase your speed each round with a 90–95% effort
on the third round.**

Individual Medley

72

Individual Medley 7A

W/U: **400** SW, **100** ST, **100** SW, **200** ST, **10 × 75** PULL (:15RI)

100	IM	(:15RI)	**300**	IM	(:15RI)
100	FR	(:15RI)	**300**	FR	(:15RI)
200	IM	(:15RI)	**400**	IM	(:15RI)
200	FR	(:15RI)	**400**	FR	(:15RI)

C/D: **300**   TOTAL: **3850**

INSTRUCTIONS: **Concentrate on descending the IMs so the last 400 IM is the fastest part of the set.**

Individual Medley

73

Individual Medley 7B

WORKOUT B

W/U: **400** SW, **100** ST, **100** SW, **200** ST, **10 × 75** PULL (:15RI)

100	IM	(:20RI)	**200**	FR	(:20RI)
100	FR	(:20RI)	**3 × 100**	IM	(:20RI)
2 × 100	IM	(:20RI)	**300**	FR	(:20RI)

C/D: **300**   TOTAL: **3050**
INSTRUCTIONS: **Concentrate on descending the IMs so the last 3 × 100 IM is the fastest part of the set.**

Individual Medley 8A

W/U: 400 SW, **3 × 200** REVERSE IM (200 K, 200 DR, 200 SW) (:20RI)

2X

2 × 100	IM K	(:15RI)	
200	IM (25 K, 25 DR)	(:15RI)	
100	50 FL, 50 BK	(:15RI)	
100	50 BK, 50 BR	(:15RI)	
100	50 BR, 50 FR	(:15RI)	
100	FR	(:30RI)	
300	IM, EVERY 3RD 25 FAST	(:30RI)	

C/D: 300 TOTAL: **3500**

INSTRUCTIONS: **Work the turns on the IM swims.**

WORKOUT A

Individual Medley 8B

WORKOUT B

W/U: **400** SW, **3 × 200** REVERSE IM (200 K, 200 DR, 200 SW) (:20RI)

			2X		
2 × 100	IM K	(:15RI)	**100**	50 BR, 50 FR	(:20RI)
100	IM DR	(:15RI)	**100**	FR	(:30RI)
100	50 FL, 50 BK	(:20RI)	**2 × 100**	IM, EVERY 2ND 25 FAST	(:30RI)
100	50 BK, 50 BR	(:20RI)			

C/D: **300**   TOTAL: **3100**

INSTRUCTIONS: **Work the turns on the IM swims.**

Individual Medley 9A

W/U: **300** FR, **300** IM (25 K, 25 DR, 25 SW), **200** FR, **200** IM (25 K, 25 DR), **100** FR, **100** IM, **6 × 75** K (ODD IM, EVEN FR DESC) (:15RI)

3 × 100 50 FL, 50 BK	(:15RI)	**300**	IM	(:20RI)
150	FR	(:10RI)	**3 × 100** 50 BR, 50 FR	(:15RI)
200	IM	(:20RI)	**150**	FR	(:10RI)
3 × 100 50 BK, 50 BR	(:15RI)	**400**	IM	(:20RI)
150	FR	(:10RI)		

C/D: **200**   TOTAL: **4100**

INSTRUCTIONS: **Moderate effort on the Free and better effort on the Stroke/IM swims.**

WORKOUT A

Individual Medley

WORKOUT B

Individual Medley 9B

W/U: **300** FR, **300** IM (25 K, 25 DR, 25 SW), **200** FR, **200** IM (25 K, 25 DR), **100** FR, **100** IM, **6 × 75** K (ODD IM, EVEN FR DESC) (:15RI)

2 × 100 50 FL, 50 BK	(:15RI)	**2 × 100** IM	(:20RI)
100 FR	(:10RI)	**2 × 100** 50 BR, 50 FR	(:15RI)
100 IM	(:20RI)	**100** FR	(:10RI)
2 × 100 50 BK, 50 BR	(:15RI)	**3 × 100** IM	(:20RI)
100 FR	(:10RI)		

C/D: **200**   TOTAL: **3350**

INSTRUCTIONS: **Moderate effort on the Free and better effort on the Stroke/IM swims.**

Individual Medley 10A

W/U: **300** FR, **200** IM K, **200** FR, **200** IM, **200** IM DR, **100** FR, **200** IM

400	FR N/S	(:20RI)	**200**	FR N/S	(:20RI)
2 × 200	IM DESC	(:20RI)	**200**	IM	(:20RI)
300	FR N/S	(:20RI)	**100**	FR N/S	(:20RI)
3 × 100	IM DESC	(:20RI)	**100**	IM FAST	

C/D: **200**   TOTAL: **3600**

INSTRUCTIONS: **Focus on changing speeds.**

WORKOUT A

79

Individual Medley 10B

WORKOUT B

W/U: **300** FR, **200** IM K, **200** FR, **200** IM, **200** IM DR, **100** FR, **200** IM

300	FR N/S	(:20RI)	**200**	IM	(:20RI)
3 × 100	IM DESC	(:20RI)	**100**	FR N/S	(:20RI)
200	FR N/S	(:20RI)	**3 × 100**	IM DESC	

C/D: **200**   TOTAL: **3000**

INSTRUCTIONS: **Focus on changing speeds.**

Stroke 1A

W/U: **150** FR, **150** BK, **150** BR, **150** FL DR

3 × 200 ST, DESC 1–3 (:30RI)

3 × 100 ST, DESC 1–3 (:20RI)

6 × 50 ST, BEST AVG (:20RI)

– 2:00 bonus rest –

400 K

– 2:00 bonus rest –

6 × 50 ST, BEST AVG (:30RI)

– 2:00 bonus rest –

6 × 150 FR (100 EASY, 50 BUILD) (:20RI)

C/D: **100** FR   TOTAL: **3500**

INSTRUCTIONS: **Change speeds during the main set.**

Stroke

81

Stroke 1B

W/U: **150** FR, **150** BK, **150** BR, **150** FL DR

2 × 200 ST, DESC 1–3	(:30RI)	– 2:00 bonus rest –
2 × 100 ST, DESC 1–3	(:20RI)	**4 × 50** ST, BEST AVG	(:30RI)
4 × 50 ST, BEST AVG	(:20RI)	– 2:00 bonus rest –
400 K		**6 × 150** FR (100 EASY, 50 BUILD)	(:20RI)
– 2:00 bonus rest –		

C/D: **100** FR   TOTAL: **3000**

INSTRUCTIONS: **Change speeds during the main set.**

Stroke 2A

W/U: **3 × 300** (100 FR, 100 IM DR, 100 K) (:15RI)

	4X			3X	
4 × 50	ST	(:15RI)	**2 × 50**	K	(:10RI)
1 × 100	IM	(:10RI)	**1 × 75**	BUILD	(:15RI)
1 × 75	EASY SW	(:30RI)	**1 × 75**	FAST	(:15RI)
	— 2:00 bonus rest —		**1 × 50**	EASY	(:30RI)

C/D: **200**   TOTAL: **3500**

INSTRUCTIONS: **Maintain good technique on the fast 75s.**

Stroke 2B

W/U: **3 × 300** (100 FR, 100 IM DR, 100 K) (:15RI)

4X		
4 × 50	ST	(:15RI)
1 × 100	IM	(:10RI)
1 × 75	EASY SW	(:30RI)

2X		
2 × 50	K	(:10RI)
1 × 75	BUILD	(:15RI)
1 × 75	FAST	(:15RI)
1 × 50	EASY	(:30RI)

– 2:00 bonus rest –

C/D: **200**   TOTAL: **3200**

INSTRUCTIONS: **Maintain good technique on the fast 75s.**

Stroke 3A

W/U: **200** SW, **200** IM K, **200** SW, **200** IM DR, **200** IM K, **100** IM DR, **200** IM SW

200	ST	(:15RI)	**2 × 100**	IM FAST	(:20RI)
2 × 100	FR	(:15RI)	**3 × 200**	ST	(:15RI)
3 × 100	IM FAST	(:20RI)	**2 × 100**	FR	(:15RI)
2 × 200	ST	(:15RI)	**1 × 100**	IM FAST	
2 × 100	FR	(:15RI)			

C/D: **300**   TOTAL: **3900**

INSTRUCTIONS: **The Stroke swims should be done with moderate effort.**

Stroke

85

Stroke 3B

WORKOUT B

W/U: **200** SW, **200** IM K, **200** SW, **200** IM DR, **100** IM K,
100 IM DR, **200** IM SW

3 × 100	ST	(:15RI)	100	IM FAST	(:30RI)
150	FR	(:15RI)	3 × 100	ST	(:15RI)
100	IM FAST	(:30RI)	150	FR	(:15RI)
2 × 100	ST	(:15RI)	100	IM FAST	(:15RI)
150	FR	(:15RI)			

C/D: **300**   TOTAL: **3050**
INSTRUCTIONS: **The Stroke swims should be done with
moderate effort.**

Stroke 4A

W/U: **300** FR, **300** IM (25 K, 25 DR, 25 SW), **3 × 100** IM (:10RI)

300	FR	(:15RI)	**4 × 75** 25 ST, 25 FR, 25 ST (:20RI)	
300	50 FR, 50 ST	(:20RI)	**300** FR	(:15RI)
300	FR	(:15RI)	**12 × 50** ST	(:20RI)
2 × 200 50 FR, 50 ST		(:20RI)	1–3 DESC	
			4–6 DESC	
300	FR	(:15RI)	7–9 DESC	
			10–12 DESC	

C/D: **300**   TOTAL: **4000**

INSTRUCTIONS: **Enjoy the Free/Stroke transitions.**

Stroke 4B

W/U: **300** FR, **300** IM (25 K, 25 DR, 25 SW), **3 × 100** IM (:10RI)

4 × 75 25 ST, 25 FR, 25 ST (:20RI)				
200 FR				(:15RI)
3 × 100 25 FR, 25 ST (:20RI)				
9 × 50 ST				(:20RI)
1–3 DESC				
4–6 DESC				
7–9 DESC				
200 FR (:15RI)				
2 × 200 50 FR, 50 ST (:20RI)				
200 FR (:15RI)				

C/D: **300**   TOTAL: **3450**

INSTRUCTIONS: **Enjoy the Free/Stroke transitions.**

Stroke

88

Stroke 5A

W/U: **100** FR, **100** (25 K, 25 DR), **200** FR, **100** (25 K, 25 DR), **300** FR, **100** (25 K, 25 DR)

3 × 300	75 ST, 75 FR	(:20RI)		**200**	ST FAST		(:40RI)
100	ST FAST		(:40RI)	**3 × 100**	25 ST, 25 FR		(:20RI)
3 × 200	50 ST, 50 FR		(:20RI)	**300**	ST FAST		

C/D: **300**   TOTAL: **3600**

INSTRUCTIONS: **Maintain good stroke technique on the longer swims.**

Stroke

89

WORKOUT B

Stroke 5B

W/U: **100** FR, **100** (25 K, 25 DR), **200** FR, **100** (25 K, 25 DR), **300** FR, **100** (25 K, 25 DR)

3 × 200	50 ST, 50 FR	(:20RI)	2 × 75	ST FAST	(:40RI)
100	ST FAST	(:40RI)	3 × 100	25 ST, 25 FR	(:20RI)
3 × 150	50 ST, 50 FR, 50 ST	(:20RI)	2 × 75	ST FAST	(:30RI)

C/D: **300**   TOTAL: **2950**

INSTRUCTIONS: **Maintain good stroke technique on the longer swims.**

Stroke

Stroke 6A

W/U: **300** SW, **200** (25 K, 25 DR), **200** (25 DR, 25 SW),
3 × 100 IM (:15RI)

3X

3 × 50	K DESC	(:10RI)
2 × 100	50 K, 50 SW	(:15RI)
150	50 FL, 50 BK, 50 BR	(:20RI)
200	ST, DESC 50s	(:30RI)

– 2:00 bonus rest –

3X

50	25 K, 25 DR	(:30RI)
50	BUILD ST	(:30RI)
50	25 DR, 25 SCULL	(:30RI)
50	FAST	(:30RI)

C/D: **300**   TOTAL: **4000**

INSTRUCTIONS: **It's OK to change strokes on each round.**

91

Stroke

Stroke 6B

WORKOUT B

W/U: **300** SW, **200** (25 K, 25 DR), **200** (25 DR, 25 SW),
3 × 100 IM (:15RI)

3 × 50 K DESC (:15RI)		
2 × 100 25 K, 25 SW (:15RI)		
150 25 FL, 25 FR, 25 BK, (:20RI) 25FR, 25 BR, 25 FR		
200 ST, DESC 50s (:30RI)		

2X		– 2:00 bonus rest –		3X
		50	25 K, 25 DR	(:30RI)
		50	BUILD ST	(:30RI)
		50	25 DR, 25 SCULL	(:30RI)
		50	FAST	(:30RI)

C/D: **300** TOTAL: **3300**

INSTRUCTIONS: **It's OK to change strokes on each round.**

Stroke 7A

W/U: **300** SW, **200** PULL, **2 × 100** IM (:10RI), **6 × 100** K (:20RI), **2 × 100** FR (:15RI), **2 × 100** IM (:15RI), **2 × 100** ST (:15RI)

10 × 100 ODD FR,
STDY EVEN ST,
BEST AVG   (2:00SI)

– 1:00 bonus rest –

10 × 50 ODD FR,
STDY EVEN ST,
BEST AVG   (1:15SI)

C/D: **300**   TOTAL: **3700**

INSTRUCTIONS: **The 50s should be done at a faster speed than the 100s.**

Stroke

Stroke 7B

W/U: **300** SW, **200** PULL, **2 × 100** IM (:10RI), **6 × 100** K (:20RI),
2 × 100 FR (:15RI), **2 × 100** IM (:15RI), **2 × 100** ST (:15RI)

4 × 100   ODD FR,
STDY EVEN ST,
BEST AVG   (:40RI)

4 × 75   ODD FR,
STDY EVEN ST,
BEST AVG
(:40RI)

4 × 50   ODD FR,
STDY EVEN ST,
BEST AVG
(:40RI)

C/D: **300**   TOTAL: **3100**
INSTRUCTIONS: **The 50s should be done at a faster speed than the 100s.**

Stroke 8A

W/U: **300** SW, **200** (25 K, 25 SW), **200** (25 DR, 25 SW), **4 × 50** IM (:10RI), **12 × 50** (50 FR, 50 IM, 50 ST/BUILD) (:15RI)

WORKOUT A

			3X
200	25 ST, 25 FR	(:20RI)	RD 1 – N/S
200	50 FR, 50 ST	(:20RI)	RD 2 – EACH 50 FASTER
200	FR	(:20RI)	RD 3 – 200 FAST
200	ST	(:30RI)	

C/D: **300** TOTAL: **4200**

INSTRUCTIONS: **It's OK to change strokes after each round.**

Stroke

Stroke 8B

W/U: **300** SW, **200** (25 K, 25 SW), **200** (25 DR, 25 SW), **4 × 50** IM
(:10RI), **12 × 50** (50 FR, 50 IM, 50 ST/BUILD) (:15RI)

	3X	
150	50 FR, 50 ST, 50 FR	(:20RI)
150	50 FR, 50 ST, 50 FR	(:20RI)
150	FR	(:20RI)
150	ST, DESC 50s	(:30RI)

C/D: **300**   TOTAL: **3600**
INSTRUCTIONS: **It's OK to change strokes after each round.**

Stroke 9A

W/U: **200** FR, **200** IM, **200** (25 ST, 25 FR),
2 × 300 (100 IM, 100 FR, 100 ST BUILD) (:20RI)

3X

100 ST, 4TH 25 FAST	(:15RI)	**100** ST, 1ST 25 FAST	(:15RI)
100 ST, 3RD 25 FAST	(:15RI)	**200** FR	(:20RI)
100 ST, 2ND 25 FAST	(:15RI)	**150** ST FAST	(:30RI)

C/D: **250**   TOTAL: **3700**
INSTRUCTIONS: **Do the first and third rounds using the same stroke.**

WORKOUT **A**

Stroke

Stroke 9B

WORKOUT B

W/U: **200** FR, **200** IM, **200** (25 ST, 25 FR),
2 × 300 (100 IM, 100 FR, 100 ST BUILD) (:20RI)

	3X		
75 ST, 3RD 25 FAST (:15RI)		**200** FR (:20RI)	
75 ST, 2ND 25 FAST (:15RI)		**125** ST FAST (:30RI)	
75 ST, 1ST 25 FAST (:15RI)			

C/D: **250** TOTAL: **3100**
INSTRUCTIONS: **Do the first and third rounds using the same stroke.**

Stroke 10A

W/U: **400** SW, **300** K, **200** DR, **100** ST, **2 × 225** [50 DR (:15RI), 100 K (:20RI), 50 BUILD ST (:20RI), 25 FAST]

3X

150	50 K, 50 D, 50 SW	(:15RI)
2 × 100	IM	(:15RI)
3 × 50	ST DESC	(:20RI)
50	FR	(:30RI)
2 × 150	ST DESC	(:20RI)

C/D: **200** TOTAL: **4200**

INSTRUCTIONS: **It's OK to change strokes after rounds.**

WORKOUT **A**

Stroke

99

Stroke 10B

W/U: **400** SW, **300** K, **200** DR, **100** ST, **2 × 225** [50 DR (:15RI),
100 K (:20RI), 50 BUILD ST (:20RI), 25 FAST]

	3X	
150	50 K, 50 D, 50 SW	(:15RI)
2 × 100	IM	(:15RI)
3 × 50	ST DESC	(:20RI)
50	FR	(:30RI)
2 × 75	ST DESC	(:20RI)

C/D: **200**   TOTAL: **3750**
INSTRUCTIONS: **It's OK to change strokes after rounds.**

About the Authors

Eric Hansen has national and international experience as a member of the U.S. National Team as an athlete and coach. Currently he is the head men's and women's swimming coach at the University of Wisconsin. In 2004 he coached an athlete who won a gold medal and set a World Record at the Olympic Games. He was also the head coach for the 2003 Pan American Games and the 2002 Short Course World Championship. Eric holds a master's degree in exercise physiology from the University of Arizona and a bachelor's degree from Iowa State University. He can be reached via e-mail at ejh@athletics.wisc.edu.

Nick Hansen holds a graduate degree in exercise physiology. He is a former U.S. National Team swimming coach, University of Wisconsin head coach, University of Arizona assistant coach, and the Loveland Master's team coach. Nick also served as an exercise physiologist at the University of Wisconsin Sports Medicine Clinic. He can be reached via e-mail at nhansen@thegroupinc.com.